HIGHER EDUCATION AND SDG17

HIGHER EDUCATION AND THE SUSTAINABLE DEVELOPMENT GOALS

Series Editor

Wendy M. Purcell, PhD FRSA
Professor with Rutgers University and Academic Research Scholar with Harvard University; Emeritus Professor and University President Emerita.

About the Series
Higher Education and the Sustainable Development Goals is a series of 17 books that address each of the SDGs in turn specifically through the lens of higher education. Adopting a solutions-based approach, each book focuses on how higher education is advancing delivery of sustainable development and the United Nations global goals.

Forthcoming Volumes
SDG16: Peace, Justice and Strong Institutions edited by Sarah E. Mendelson

Higher Education and the Sustainable Development Goals

HIGHER EDUCATION AND SDG17

Partnerships for the Goals

EDITED BY

ÁNGEL CABRERA
Georgia Institute of Technology, USA

AND

DREW CUTRIGHT
Georgia Institute of Technology, USA

emerald PUBLISHING

United Kingdom – North America – Japan – India
Malaysia – China

Emerald Publishing Limited
Howard House, Wagon Lane, Bingley BD16 1WA, UK

First edition 2023

British Library Cataloguing in Publication Data
A catalogue record for this book is available from the British Library

ISBN: 978-1-80455-707-5 (Print)
ISBN: 978-1-80455-704-4 (Online)
ISBN: 978-1-80455-706-8 (Epub)

To Tom Lovejoy, scientist, teacher, change maker, and friend.

PRAISE FOR *HIGHER EDUCATION AND SDG17*

"This is a timely book, which will provide concrete support to the debate on SDG17 and on the actions the higher education community should take in order to pursue its implementation."

Walter Leal, Professor of Environment and Technology, Manchester Metropolitan University, Series Editor of *Concise Guides to the United Nations Sustainable Development Goals* (Emerald)

"As a book series, *Higher Education and the SDGs* will make an important contribution to accelerating delivery against the global goals. To start the series with the book on Partnerships for the Goals makes perfect sense and is highly symbolic since accomplishing the sixteen other ones largely depends on cooperation and collaboration among all relevant stakeholders. This book impressively shows the important role of higher education in teaming up with actors from various other sectors to meet the ambitious aims of the Agenda 2030 collectively."

Prof. Andreas Kaplan, ESCP Business School, Sorbonne Alliance

"The book series *Higher Education and the SDGs* will make a valuable contribution to policy dialogue and higher education practices in achieving the SDGs. This first book in the series on Higher Education for Partnerships for the Goals highlights a range of partnerships, discusses some successful partnership cases and explores ways to enhance the impact of higher education partnerships to accelerate progress towards SDGs."

Qudsia Kalsoom, University of Dundee, UK.

CONTENTS

LIST OF FIGURES AND TABLES

FIGURES

TABLES

ABOUT THE CONTRIBUTORS

Srijan Banik is the Founder and Director of the Social Impact Lab, BRAC University where he works jointly with the students and faculty members to mentor the change-makers of his campus to initiate different impact projects. Along with that, he is also a Global Fellow at the Open Society University Network (OSUN). He is a senior student studying Computer Science and Engineering at BRAC University, a creative thinker, and a youth advocate. In 2021 he became a Millennium Fellow and led the very first cohort of Millennium Fellows at BRACU as its Campus Director. He has worked in a wide range of fields like teaching robotics, combating the food traceability problem, and climate change. He has been actively working on advancing SDGs 3, 4, and 13 with his Start-up KriShop and Civic Engagement project Alokdhenu. He also runs a Podcast that lets Young Leaders from all over the world share their stories.

Marilyn A. Brown is a Regents' Professor at Georgia Tech and a Joint Faculty Member at Oak Ridge National Laboratory, where she worked for many years. She created and co-leads the Climate and Energy Policy Lab and the Master of Sustainable Energy and Environmental Management program. Her research focuses on the design and modelling of energy and carbon reduction policies and energy market transitions. She contributed to the Intergovernmental Panel on Climate Change reports that shared the 2007 Nobel Peace Prize. During her eight years as a Presidential appointee to the Board of Directors of the Tennessee Valley Authority, 18 coal units were closed, one nuclear unit was completed, and many virtual power plants of energy efficiency were built. She served two terms on the DOE Electricity Advisory Committee, has written nine books on clean energy and climate, and is a member of the National Academies of Engineering and Sciences.

Ángel Cabrera is the President of the Georgia Institute of Technology, one of America's leading research universities. Prior to this, he led George Mason University (Virginia's largest public university), Thunderbird School of Global Management (now part of Arizona State University), and IE Business School in Madrid. He was the Lead Author of the UN Global Compact 'Principles for Responsible Management Education' (PRME) and a Co-founder of the University Global Coalition, a network of universities partnering with the United Nations in support of the Sustainable Development Goals. He serves on the Boards of the National Geographic Society, Harvard College Visiting Committee, and Bankinter Innovation Foundation in Spain. He has served on the Board of the Federal Reserve Bank of Richmond and three public companies. An alumnus of Georgia Tech and Universidad Politécnica of Madrid, he was named a Young Global Leader by the World Economic Forum, a Great Immigrant by the Carnegie Corporation of New York and H. Crown Fellow by the Aspen Institute and has received honorary degrees from Miami Dade College and Universidad Politécnica of Madrid.

María Cortés Puch is Vice President at the Sustainable Development Solutions Network (SDSN), where she leads its efforts to build a global network of universities, research centres, and civil society organizations that pursue sustainable development locally through research, public education, executive training, convening of social stakeholders, and incubation of solutions. She represents the SDSN as Commissioner to the Pathfinder Lancet Commission and co-leads the SDSN Europe, an initiative to support the alignment of European policies with the SDGs and the Paris Climate Agreement, contributing to its publications, including the 2021 Europe Sustainable Development Report. She co-edited the 2020 SDSN guide *Accelerating Education for the SDGs in Universities*.

Jasmine Crowe is an Award-winning Social Entrepreneur, TED Speaker, and the Founder and CEO of Goodr, a sustainable Food Waste Management Company that leverages technology to combat hunger and food waste. In 2017, after years of feeding people experiencing homelessness from her kitchen, she launched Goodr, which has redirected over 5 million pounds of surplus food from restaurants, event centres, airports, and businesses to the millions of food insecure people. She is the Author of the children's book, *Everybody Eats*, an inspirational story about fighting hunger. She has been featured on CNBC, *Oprah Magazine,* Inc., *Forbes,* Fast Co., and the *New York Times*. In addition, *Entrepreneur Magazine* named her as one of the top 100 influential female founders. She is Co-chair of the Drawdown Georgia Leadership Council, and Goodr was a Founding Member of the Drawdown Georgia Business Compact.

Drew Cutright is a Senior Strategy Consultant in Georgia Institute of Technology's Office of Strategic Consulting, with a focus on international initiatives and sustainability. She is the Program Director for the University Global Coalition, a global network of universities working in partnership with the United Nations in support of its Sustainable Development Goals. Prior to joining Georgia Tech, she held roles as a sustainable building consultant, environmental planner, and environmental educator. She has a Master's in Environmental Planning and Design and a Bachelor of Arts in English Language and Literature.

Shriya Dayal is a Master's Student in Transnational Governance at the European University Institute with a deep interest in the UN Sustainable Development Goals, especially SDG17. She has had the opportunity to work on sustainability education in the private sector, climate change education in schools, and circular economy innovation in universities. She aims to contribute towards solving global policy problems by strengthening partnerships between transnational actors. She is also a Millennium Fellow from the class of 2021 and served as the Campus Director of her cohort at Punjab Engineering College, India during her bachelor's degree.

Susan T. L. Harrison is Deputy Vice-Chancellor: Research and Internationalisation at UCT and a Bioprocess Engineer focused on nature-based solutions in sustainable development. Her portfolio includes advancing the research quality, quantity, and impact across the university; enhancing UCT's African agenda; internationalization and research partnerships; growing and transforming the postgraduate sector; and oversight of interdisciplinary university research institutes. She has led research groupings and championed interdisciplinary research capacity at UCT, as well as the role of soft-funded researchers. Her contribution to research and innovation nationally has been demonstrated through her leadership role in the nurturing of innovation and in the implementation plans for the bioeconomy strategy. She has co-authored 255 research papers including 163 refereed journals, 81 conference proceedings, and 11 book chapters. She has supervised 136 postgraduate students to completion. She is a Fellow of the South African Academy of Engineers and a Member of the USA National Academy of Engineers, being the 6th from Africa elected to membership.

Tahl S. Kestin is the Network Manager for the Sustainable Development Solutions Network Regional Network for Australia, New Zealand and Pacific (SDSN AusNZPac), hosted by the Monash Sustainable Development Institute at Monash University, Australia. She works with SDSN member institutions and a range of local and global organizations to help mobilize the university sector on the SDGs. She led the writing of the 2017 guide *Getting Started with the SDGs in Universities* and the 2020 SDSN guide *Accelerating Education for the SDGs in Universities*. She also leads the joint SDSN AusNZPac and Australasian Campuses Towards Sustainability (ACTS) forum series, *Accelerating SDGs Practice*, which aims to help member institutions accelerate and scale up action on the SDGs.

John A. Lanier is the Executive Director of the Ray C. Anderson Foundation, a Georgia-based private family foundation honouring the legacy of the late Ray C. Anderson. Ray, John's grandfather, was the Founder and CEO of Interface, Inc., the world's largest manufacturer of carpet tile and a leading company committed to environmental sustainability. The foundation funds multiple environmental initiatives, including the Ray C. Anderson Center for Sustainable Business in Georgia Tech's Scheller College of Business, a sustainable highway and transportation initiative called 'The Ray', the Ray of Hope Prize in partnership with The Biomimicry

Institute, the Drawdown Georgia initiative, the Georgia Climate Project, and the Global Change Program at Georgia Tech. He shares his late grandfather's passion for Earth and her natural systems, and he is the Author of *Mid-Course Correction Revisited*, an updated edition of his grandfather's first book.

Julio Lumbreras, PhD, Eng, MPA, is Associate Professor at the Technical University of Madrid (UPM) and Visiting Scientist at Harvard T.H. Chan School of Public Health, where he is the Instructor of the course 'Sustainable Cities'. He was a Member of the Board of the European Mission for 'Climate-neutral and smart cities'. He is now part of the Net Zero Cities consortium, and he is leading the multi-stakeholder platform for the implementation of the mission in Spain. He is Founding Associate Editor in the *Open Access Journal on Frontiers in Sustainable Cities*. He is Co-author of more than 80 papers and books on air quality, climate change, sustainable cities, and higher education. He Co-edited the 2020 SDSN guide *Accelerating Education for the SDGs in Universities*. He is passionate about increasing sustainability in higher education, turning universities into key agents to systemically transform cities towards sustainability.

Luz Patricia Montaño-Salinas' professional career has developed between Information Technology Management and Internationalization. During her 29 years at Tecnológico de Monterrey, she has collaborated in academics as well as in administrative posts, always related to the international development of the university. She obtained two Master's degrees, an MBA from EGADE Business School with specialization in Global e-Management and a Master in Information Technologies Management, both at Tecnológico de Monterrey. She has been a Speaker at several international conferences. As Director for International Innovation and Networks at Tecnológico de Monterrey, she is responsible for designing new formats for students' international experiences and new paths for the university's internationalization as well as university activities at consortia like Universitas21, APRU, ECIU, HUC, and CINDA, among other duties. She is currently a PhD student at University of Hull in the UK.

Ayushi Nahar hails from the Silicon Valley of India and is currently an undergraduate student pursuing her law degree at Jindal Global Law School, O.P. Jindal Global University, India. She aims to optimally use her legal education to empower herself, and by extension empower those who were not provided with similar opportunities. She has a strong foundational base in finance and investments. She was recently awarded the United Nations Millennium Fellowship for her work in the field of financial literacy. Within the law and justice segment, she assisted in organizing a panel meeting in collaboration with the Department of Justice, India that was aimed at brainstorming the integration of technology and AI in the justice domain. She is a Tech Law Geek and shares a keen penchant towards reading about work focused on the human DNA and gene editing. Additionally, she is a Professional Kathak Dancer who has performed at various national events, an Articulate Writer and Debater, a Researcher with experience, and an Avid Reader. She lives by the following quote from her favourite book, *All The Light We Cannot See* by Anthony Doerr – 'Open your eyes and see what you can with them before they close forever'.

Joanna Newman, MBE FRSA, is Chief Executive and Secretary General of the Association of Commonwealth Universities (ACU) – the world's oldest international network of universities, dedicated to building a better world through higher education. Through international collaboration, the ACU brings universities together to advance knowledge, promote understanding, broaden minds, and improve lives. The ACU champions higher education as a cornerstone of stronger societies, supporting its members, partners, and stakeholders as they adapt to a changing world. She represents the ACU on the United Nations Sustainable Development Solutions Network's Leadership Council and the High-level Advisory Group for Mission 4.7. She is a Lay Member of the Council of Cardiff University and sits on the Board of the Council for At-Risk Academics (CARA). Her previous roles included the Vice-Principal (International) at King's College London, Director of the UK Higher Education International Unit (now known as Universities UK International), and Head of Higher Education at the British Library. She is a Senior Research Fellow in History at King's College London.

Her most recent publication is *Nearly the New World: The British West Indies and the Flight From Nazism, 1933–1945.*

Michael Oxman is the Managing Director of the Ray C. Anderson Center for Sustainable Business and a Professor of the Practice who has worked in industry, nonprofits, government, and academia over the course of his career with a range of domestic and international engagements. In addition to work in political risk and financial valuations, he has spent much of his career focused on corporate sustainability and social license to operate in both the United States and across many international locations. At the Ray C. Anderson Center for Sustainable Business, he helps to lead (along with the Faculty Director and Center staff) a number of initiatives including the recently launched Drawdown Georgia Business Compact (focused on carbon reduction in Georgia through a just and sustainable transition). He also teaches a consulting-based practicum course with companies of all sizes that focuses on corporate sustainability topics while leveraging best practices in problem-solving approaches.

José Manuel Páez-Borrallo is Vice Rector for International Affairs at Tecnológico de Monterrey. Prior to that, he was Dean of the School of Telecommunications Engineering at Universidad Politécnica de Madrid (UPM), Vice President for International Relations, and President's Delegate at RCC in Harvard University. He has also been Visiting Professor at Universidade de Sao Paulo, as well as Visiting Senior Researcher at International Computer Science Institute (ICSI) and Berkeley Wireless Research Centre (BWRC) at University of California, Berkeley. He has worked in the private sector in Germany and has created and supported several start-ups. Among his contributions to internationalization in higher education, he led the creation of the permanent delegations of UPM abroad in China, USA, and Brazil, and was Founder, President, and current Honorary President of Magalhães Network.

Professor Maano Ramutsindela is Dean of the Faculty of Science at UCT and a Human Geographer. Having obtained his PhD in Geography as a Conon Collins Scholar from Royal Holloway,

University of London, he has received numerous awards, including South Africa's National Research Foundation (NRF) Award for the Transformation of the Science Cohort, the NRF President's Award, a Mandela Fellow of the W.E.B Du Bois Institute for African and African American Research (Harvard University), Distinguished Hubert H. Humphrey Visiting Chair at Macalester College, a Fellow of the Society of South African Geographers, and a Member of the Academy of Science of South Africa. He is the Founding Co-chair of the Worldwide Universities Network Global Africa Group. His research focuses on the intersection of society and nature, and this theme runs through his latest books: *The Violence of Conservation in Africa: State, Militarization and Alternatives* (co-edited with Matose & Mushonga, 2022) and the *Routledge Handbook of Development and Environment* (co-edited with McCusker, Ahmed, & Solís, 2022).

Roy Richards's professional experience has been in General Management and Board Leadership of companies and nonprofits. He began serving on corporate and NGO boards in his early 20's and took over his family's manufacturing company as CEO at age 28. He still chairs it today (southwire.com: $7B+ revenues and 6,000+ employees). His philanthropic work is focused on American ecology: He co-founded an environmental advocacy nonprofit to protect Georgia's coastal land and waters (onehundredmiles.org), started a venture fund for climate change communications initiatives in the southeastern USA (1earth.fund), and created a private fund to finance high priority land protection in the southeastern USA (terrahconservationcapital.com). He is an Adjunct Professor of the practice at the Georgia Tech Scheller College of Business and Co-chair of the Drawdown Georgia Leadership Council.

Nikhil Seth is the Executive Director of the United Nations Institute for Training and Research. Before this post in 2015, he was the Director of the Division for Sustainable Development, Department of Economic and Social Affairs (DESA) at the United Nations Secretariat. During his United Nation (UN) career, he has served as Special Assistant and Chief of Office to the Under-Secretary-General for Economic and Social Affairs, Chief of the Policy Coordination

Branch in the Division for ECOSOC Support and Coordination, Secretary of the Economic and Social Council (ECOSOC) and the Second Committee of the General Assembly, and Director of the DESA Office for ECOSOC Support and Coordination. Before joining the UN, he was a delegate to the UN in the Permanent Mission of India to the UN and a Member of the Indian Diplomatic Service. Prior to this, he worked as a Lecturer in Economics in St. Stephen College, Delhi University. He holds a Masters in Economics from Delhi University.

L. Beril Toktay is the Brady Family Chaired Professor of Operations Management, Regents' Professor, the Faculty Director of the Ray C. Anderson Center for Sustainable Business at the Georgia Tech Scheller College of Business, and the Interim Executive Director of the Brook Byers Institute for Sustainable Systems. A Distinguished Fellow of the INFORMS Manufacturing and Service Operations Management Society, her research focuses on sustainable operations and supply chain management. She has co-developed Award-winning Interdisciplinary Educational Programs such as Serve-Learn-Sustain, which offers students academic opportunities to advance sustainable communities, and the Carbon Reduction Challenge, a competition focused on empowering students to become part of the climate change solution. The Metro Atlanta Chamber of Commerce selected her as a 2019 E3 Impact Award Finalist, an award that recognizes 'visionary individuals advancing sustainability in Atlanta'.

Sam Vaghar is a Social Entrepreneur committed to helping young people use their voices and power to make a difference. With 15 years of impact Co-founding and Leading Millennium Campus Network (MCN), he has helped launch the Millennium Fellowship: a student movement for the UN Sustainable Development Goals at 200 campuses worldwide. He has given talks at over 100 institutions worldwide, including at Harvard University, MIT, the White House, the United Nations, the Vatican, and on speaking tours across four nations for the U.S. Department of State. He earned a Bachelor of Arts Degree from Brandeis University and a Master in Public Administration (MPA) degree from the Kennedy

School of Government at Harvard University. He has received two Honorary Degrees and also served as Commencement Speaker at Monmouth College in 2020. His work, writing, and contributions have been spotlighted by *The Boston Globe*, CNN, Fast Company, and more publications.

Summer Wyatt-Buchan has pursued studies in Climate Change and Sustainability with a focus on raising awareness of the need for climate action. She has worked through social movements and campaigns for corporate environmental accountability and a liveable future in her role as Director of Sustainability Analysts at Voiz Academy. She has also led 20 fellows in developing their own social impact initiatives through her role as Campus Director in the Millennium Fellowship 2021. She recently completed a Climate & Health Fellowship with Planet Reimagined where she co-authored a paper. She looks to be in a professional field whereby she can better ensure a wider contribution to meeting the United Nations Sustainable Development Goals. She is undertaking her MSc in Environment, Politics and Society at University College London (UCL).

HESDG17 SERIES EDITOR – PREFACE

Professor Wendy M. Purcell, PhD FRSA

Higher education (HE) is making an important contribution to delivery of the Sustainable Development Goals (SDGs). Through high quality teaching and learning, HE supports the development of responsible citizens as scholars, leaders, entrepreneurs, and professionals. Universities and colleges undertake socially impactful research to help find solutions for the world's most pressing issues. They are also active in civic and community settings as anchor institutions. Nevertheless, given the fierce urgency of (un)sustainable development, the climate crisis and widening inequity within countries and across the globe, HE needs to do more and go faster. For HE to deliver fully against the SDGs, it needs to adapt to this shared global agenda for transformative change.

This book series focuses on the role of HE in advancing the SDGs, identifying some successes to date and opportunities ahead. In sharing the ways and means universities and colleges across the world are engaging with the SDGs, the series seeks to both inspire and enable those in the HE sector and stakeholders beyond to channel their efforts towards solutions for the grand challenges represented by the global goals. Insights gleaned from relevant case studies, innovations, reflective accounts, and student stories can help the HE sector both deepen and accelerate its engagement with the SDGs. Each book seeks to capture ways HE is fulfilling its contribution to delivery of the goal at hand and its underlying targets. Illustrating the work of students, that undertaken by faculty and staff of the institution and conducted with others, positions HE as a change agent operating at a systems level to help to create a world that leaves no one behind.

Taking up this global challenge, SDG17 'Partnerships for the Goals' is a call for radical collaboration of HE with local, national, and international actors. HE is well-suited to partnership working with those in health, business, and community settings. Bringing key assets of curiosity and the pursuit of truth to partners seeking solutions and driving innovation, universities and colleges operate in global knowledge networks. Helping realize human potential connects the worlds of learning and work and entrepreneurship in support of inclusive economic growth. As place-makers, HE institutions can use their convening power to draw stakeholders around a problem in support of the adaptive change needed to tackle the challenges of sustainable development.

This book on HE and SDG17 acknowledges the relative ease with which universities and colleges network with one another across the world, share their research findings, and support the aspirations of talented students and faculty. Academic freedom includes the opportunity to work without borders *within* the academy. However, working *beyond* HE with local and global stakeholders calls for new models of learning, research, leadership, and governance essential to the pursuit of the SDGs. The longer time horizons HE works across together with the regular refresh of its student body enables universities and colleges to withstand short-term political and business cycles. As such, HE can support the development of trustful relationship building necessary to support effective partnership working. The need for HE to deliver on its academic mission and share knowledge and learning, within the classroom and through the academic literature, demands transparency of purpose and outcomes in collaborative ventures. Together with shared place-based agenda for health of people, planet, and shared prosperity, HE can be both an effective partner and a vehicle for partnership. For example, climate action in cities brings a HE institution into relationship with civic and community leaders, with businesses and healthcare providers. So too, in communities transitioning from old world industries to the new world of the green economy, universities and colleges are central to the partnerships effecting a just transition.

This book is clear that without the full participation of HE, delivery of the SDGs will be materially compromised. But to sustain the current level of activity and pursue the deeper engagement needed, HE itself needs to tackle the actual and perceived barriers to more fulsome and complex models of collaboration. From acknowledging the work involved in creating and sustaining a partnership in staff workload models and faculty portfolios for tenure, to more easily deploying students into community settings to work on social projects and crediting their work, HE needs to change its quantum of activity in this space. Indeed, as this book acknowledges, HE needs to reach out to all those who can benefit from what it offers and do so in a way that engages the public. Moving from an ivory tower model of a university or college to one that represents an institution connected to those it serves calls for more innovation in partnership models, recognizing many of those developed to date reinforce inequity and models of colonialism.

As noted in this book, the COVID-19 pandemic accelerated change within HE and advanced partnerships across the academy globally. Marshalling the intellectual, physical, and human assets of universities and colleges was central to vaccine development and healthcare delivery programs in community settings. As such, an important legacy of the pandemic is the new partnership assets developed within HE and relationship capital that can now be deployed to progress the SDGs with a renewed sense of urgency. From global classrooms to new public–private partnerships, this book shows that HE has the wherewithal to make a deeper and wider contribution to the goals and to do so at a pace demanded by the scale of the sustainable development challenges now and ahead. This relies on explicit strategic intention by HE institutions and being invitational to students, faculty, staff, and those in the wider stakeholder ecosystem.

This book highlights the enormous untapped potential for HE to create partnerships for the goals and in doing so advance the frontiers of knowledge that in turn drive up institutional reach and reputation. Immersive engagement with the SDGs can catalyze pedagogic innovation, serve to refresh curricula, and stimulate new program development. It can also open new avenues for research, attract new sources of funding, and energize people to deliver on the academic mission. Developing the next generation and creating the technology and insights to tackle the issues of social justice in our communities, social impact work is the business of HE. It is clear that HE needs to be a full partner in partnerships for the goals – the task ahead is for HE to realize this mission. In adopting the SDGs, the academy can help create the conditions within and beyond the institution to deliver on the betterment of all humankind.

ACKNOWLEDGEMENTS

First and foremost, a monumental thank you to the authors in this book, for taking the time to share their insights with the broader higher education community and, most importantly, for their courageous leadership in steering our universities towards greater impact.

To Wendy and the team at Emerald – for cheering us on and guiding us – both were needed!

To our colleagues and friends at Georgia Tech – some of the most supportive, creative, and kindest colleagues we have known. And to our colleagues and friends in the University Global Coalition, who inspire us daily and encourage us to keep doing what we can to build a more inclusive and sustainable world.

Ángel thanks the many colleagues who have helped shape his thinking and inspired his actions, especially Prof. Tom Lovejoy, who passed away in 2021 after a long, productive and inspiring life committed to using science to build a better world. Drew thanks her mom Carol, sister Kyle, partner Daniel, and the friends she is lucky enough to consider family.

1

INTRODUCTION

Ángel Cabrera and Drew Cutright

The choice is not between wild places or people; it is between a rich or an impoverished existence for Man. (Thomas E. Lovejoy, 1941–2021)

The riches tapped by the industrial revolution have come at a dear price. We live longer, healthier, safer lives than any prior generation. Yet the innovations that made this possible also originated a set of complex challenges which threaten major human harm if not the very viability of our way of life. Under the auspices of the United Nations (UN), governments from around the world have adopted a framework, the Sustainable Development Goals (SDGs), articulating a call to action for all sectors and nations to join forces to find an equitable, sustainable, and inclusive way forward that will lift the lives of all people without causing irreparable damage to the planet we inhabit.

Universities have the capacity to play a major role in this quest. Given the magnitude of the challenges we face, they should accept their responsibility to do their part. Universities educate the professionals, scientists, and decision-makers who shape all areas of human activity. They carry out research to understand the challenges we face, develop new technologies, and propose new solutions. Universities are also trusted convenors of other actors.

They frame problems and amplify ideas, influence the thinking of decision-makers, and bring multiple stakeholders to the table. The goal of this book is to explore how universities can most effectively use their convening power to form effective partnerships, among themselves and with other actors, to maximize their collective impact in bringing us closer to achieving the SDGs.

In discussing the urgent challenges articulated by the SDGs, it is important to acknowledge the incalculable benefits yielded by 200 years of technological innovation and commerce. Indeed, over the span of just 10 generations, humans experienced a leap in quality of life unlike any other period in history. We now live more than twice as long and are more than 10 times wealthier than our ancestors were at the dawn of the nineteenth century, while our population has grown by almost eightfold.

In the early nineteenth century, the average human had to make ends meet on the equivalent of $3 per day in today's money, compared to more than $40 today – and close to $150 in places like the USA, Canada, and Australia. Back then, not even the very wealthiest could buy necessities we now take for granted, such as life-saving medicines and vaccines. In Europe alone, before the advent of modern vaccines, half a million people may have died from smallpox every year, in addition to the countless others who went blind or suffered crippling long-term sequelae. Average life expectancy today has surpassed 70 years, having consistently hovered below 30 since our hunter-gatherer days, and through the Neolithic Age, until the onset of the Industrial Revolution.

Today, about 90% of males and more than 80% of females can read, compared to one in 10 people before the nineteenth century (World Economic Forum, 2022). A transatlantic flight today costs less than a fifth of a boat passage in the eighteenth century, which could last more than a month if it made it to the other end. Health, education, travel, leisure, entertainment, nutrition, culture, safety, every aspect of human life has been transformed in about two centuries. And while it took 300,000 years for humans to colonize the entire planet and reach our first billion, these new technologies propelled the human population to 6 billion by the end of the twentieth century. As we write this, the UN estimates that the world population has just crossed 8 billion.

This spectacular progress was not easy. The dramatic change in agriculture and manufacturing, urbanization, capital formation, and global trade caused deadly class struggles, economic and social inequality, revolution, violence, pollution, and destructive warfare on a scale never seen before.

At every step we (humans) were forced to find new solutions. We created new technologies that resolved deficiencies of earlier ones. We developed organizational models that made us more productive and work, less onerous. We experimented with political regimes as we found systems of government that did a better job spreading the newfound wealth and keeping us safer, healthier, and better educated. We created ever more sophisticated systems of mutual support like private insurance and public social security, welfare, and health care. We created international alliances and new systems of global trade and finance, cooperation, and conflict resolution. We cleaned up cities and rivers and curbed air pollution.

Yet the magnitude of our population growth, the speed of change, and our insatiable thirst for natural resources outpaced our capacity to adapt and our planet's ability to regenerate. It also exacerbated inequality between and within nations. Because of accidents of geography and history, the new technologies and trade relations benefitted and empowered some more than others. And while the environmental issues that were created affected all, the wealthy were relatively better protected to withstand the damage; those who benefitted the least became the most vulnerable.

According to the IMF's 2022 World Inequality Report, the poorer half of the world's adults today have a net worth of about 2,900 euros (in purchasing power parity terms) and earn 8.5% of all available income, while the richest 10% are 190 times wealthier and earn more than half of all world income (International Monetary Fund, 2022). The UN estimates that about 1 billion people live in slums or informal settlements – mostly in Asia and sub-Saharan Africa – thus facing debilitating health and safety risks and barriers of access to economic opportunity and education. In our own city of Atlanta – a modern, thriving transportation, commerce, and technology hub in the one of the wealthiest nations in the world – the poorest 20% households live on less than $10,000 per year, while the richest 20% makes more than $255,000.

The industrial revolution that produced so much wealth and progress was powered by abundant and cheap energy in the form of fossil fuels. As we would eventually learn, however, the CO_2 that is pumped into the atmosphere from combusting fossil fuels is excellent at retaining infrared radiation and therefore increasing the average temperature of our planet. Higher average temperatures mean smaller icecaps and glaciers, higher sea levels that threaten human coastal settlements, and changes in climate patterns that affect the availability of fresh water, increase the frequency of fires and destructive storms, disturb agriculture and fisheries, and accelerate the destruction of biological diversity. Meanwhile, growing demand for food by a larger and wealthier population pushes deforestation to make room for crops and pastures, thus debilitating the capacity of our forests to absorb CO_2 and accentuating global warming. Overfishing and deforestation, coupled with higher average temperatures and the acidification of oceans, further disturbs the balance of ecosystems on land and under water and destroys biological diversity.

Not all humans contributed equally to this problem. Wealthy countries are responsible for most of the world's historical carbon emissions. Even today, the richest 1% owns 38% of global wealth, makes 19% of all global income, and is responsible for 17% of CO_2 emissions (International Monetary Fund, 2022). The average American today is about 32 times wealthier than the average Nigerian, consumes 84 times more electricity, and emits 27 times more CO_2. Because we all share the same atmosphere, oceans, and climate systems, both rich and poor suffer the consequences of these externalities. Yet it is becoming increasingly evident that poorer nations, and poorer areas within wealthier nations, are more vulnerable than those who benefitted the most and contributed the most to the problem.

As we write this, world leaders are gathered in Egypt for the 27th UN climate change conference (COP27). Six years ago, the same world leaders agreed in Paris to do everything possible to keep average world temperatures within 1.5° of pre-industrial levels. To achieve that goal, carbon emissions would need to be cut in half by 2030. Yet emissions have so far gone up, not down, and it seems increasingly clear that we will miss the Paris target.

According to the UN Intergovernmental Panel on Climate Change (IPCC), the difference between 1.5° and 2° could mean hundreds of millions more lives and livelihoods upended by higher seas. The most vulnerable countries now demand so-called 'loss and damage' compensation from industrialized countries for the harm they have caused – a Tragedy of the Commons of global proportions.

That is the conundrum that our species faces. How to continue to drive economic prosperity and human development for everyone without depleting the regenerative capacity of our planet or heating it up beyond repair.

In 2015, the United Nations General Assembly adopted the SDGs as a shared framework for collective action that recognizes the severity and urgency of the situation and the complexity of the solutions that will be required. The framework is structured around 17 broadly defined Global Goals that highlight both the multidimensionality of the challenges that we face as well as the underlying interdependencies.

The SDGs pledge to end poverty and hunger, improve health and education, and reduce inequality, especially in places and communities that have been left behind. That will require that we incorporate more people into the modern economy, that we drive economic growth while reducing carbon emissions, and that we grow in a way that safeguards the health of land and marine ecosystems.

Dividing this complex web of objectives and interdependences into 17 discrete goals (or any other number for that matter) is a thankless and somewhat arbitrary exercise. There are many ways to dissect, group, and label the challenges we face, each approach highlighting specific angles and causal links at the expense of making others less obvious. Yet, by agreeing on a specific framework and then developing concrete metrics and targets around it, we develop a shared language, we increase transparency and accountability, we inspire action, we track progress more effectively, and we make it easier to align efforts by different actors in different geographies.

This last benefit of the SDGs is critical. Sustainable development is multidimensional, multidisciplinary, multistakeholder, and multinational. It requires not only a multitude of efforts by a multitude of actors, but that those actors coordinate efforts and complement one another. In other words, partnerships are essential in achieving the goals, and that is why one of the 17 goals, SDG17, is dedicated precisely to forming partnerships for development.

Because we're locked-in by decades of capital and human investment, of path-dependent institutional arrangements around fossil fuels – combustion and jet engines, roads and railroads, ports and airports, gas stations, coal plants – solutions require not only new technologies but new capabilities, policies, business models, and market incentives (Unruh, 2000). Because energy and food markets, our atmosphere, our oceans, our rivers, and our climate are shared across national boundaries, any intervention will need to be coordinated globally. And because any global change will carry uneven effects to people in different geographies and circumstances, issues of human development and economic opportunity need to be addressed simultaneously.

To achieve viable solutions, we need scientists and engineers galore. But also responsible business leaders, entrepreneurs working on new solutions at the local level, and multinationals willing to change the way they do business at large scale. We need local, regional, and national policy-makers, financial institutions that distribute cost and risk effectively, diplomats who can craft new cooperative arrangements, non-governmental organizations filling the gaps markets cannot reach, and communicators and educators who inspire and empower all of us to do our part.

SDG17 highlights the need for partnerships that bridge sectors, stakeholders, disciplines, and national interests, that allow professionals to collaborate and solutions to spread. More specifically, SDG17 calls for partnerships of various types: multistakeholder partnerships around voluntary commitments, global trade arrangements that liberalize trade and bring the benefits of commerce to more markets in an environmentally responsible way, partnerships to provide new models of financing for development, partnerships to advance scientific data and develop new research capabilities, partnerships to develop technical capabilities where needed, to advance and spread technology.

When we combine these two requirements for achieving the Global Goals, the need for new skills and attitudes among professionals and decision-makers, with the need to form effective partnerships, the role of universities becomes evident.

Universities, by their very nature, educate professionals in all areas of human endeavour. They train scientists and engineers, business and policy leaders, teachers and communicators, innovators, problem solvers, and critical thinkers. According to the World Bank, 40% of the college aged population around the world is enrolled in college (though the numbers dip to single digits in sub-Saharan Africa and other low-income countries) (World Bank, 2022). If we have any hope that new generations of professionals understand the urgency of the SDGs, develop the capabilities and attitudes necessary to address them, and accept their own personal responsibility, universities need to make it a priority to embed the SDGs into their mission, their curriculum, and their ethos.

Some universities also discharge important responsibilities in the area of research. In the United States, for example, universities spent $86 billion in 2020 in research and development according to the National Science Foundation (2022). This accounts for about 12% of total R&D expenditures in the country, and more than the 9% of the research conducted directly by government research centres. While the business sector is responsible for about three quarters of the national research enterprise, their focus on commercially viable solutions leaves the bulk of basic scientific research in the hand of our universities. If we have any chance at identifying new breakthroughs in sustainable energy production, storage and distribution, sustainable agriculture, environmental protection, infectious diseases, and other areas central to human development, it is of paramount importance that universities align their research enterprises with the challenges articulated by the SDGs.

Lastly, universities are natural convenors of other actors and stakeholders. They strive to create multidisciplinary environments that are driven by curiosity and the exchange of knowledge, are welcoming of dissent and informed debate, and are therefore uniquely suited to act as trusted convenors of other actors.

Universities have unfortunately been slow to accept their institutional responsibility to take part in the global effort towards sustainable development. During the last global development framework, the so-called Millennium Development Goals (2000–2015), the institutional engagement of universities was modest at best. While individual faculty members played important roles as experts and thought leaders, universities rarely adopted the framework institutionally, and their voice was seldom heard at global gatherings.

There are promising signs that things may be improving. A good example is the Principles of Responsible Management Education (PRME), established in 2007. Working as a Senior Advisor to the UN Global Compact, one of us, Ángel Cabrera, at the time President of the Thunderbird School of Global Management, chaired a Global Committee of Business Educators that drafted six principles now endorsed by hundreds of institutions worldwide. The principles committed signatory schools to incorporate global citizenship and responsibility in teaching, curriculum design, and research, to play an active role in convening other actors, and to partner with one another. With support from leading business school accrediting bodies (most notably AACSB and EFMD) and other organizations, PRME now has chapters around the world, organizes events to share best practices, supports the exchange of resources, and publicizes the progress being made.

During the 2012 UN Conference on Sustainable Development in Brazil (Rio+20), PRME partnered with UN DESA and other UN organizations to launch the Higher Education Sustainability Initiative (HESI). HESI organizes an annual High Level Political Forum focused on the role of universities in achieving sustainable development and offers tools like Sulitest to promote sustainability literacy around the world.

Also in 2012, Columbia University Professor Jeffrey Sachs, in partnership with the UN Secretary General, launched the Sustainable Development Solutions Network (SDSN), a non-profit organization with a membership of more than 1,700 institutions organized in 50 networks across 144 countries that fosters knowledge generation and exchange, offers open-access learning materials, data and reports, and promotes solutions to advance the SDGs (UN-SDSN, *About*). One of this volume's chapters discusses high-level learnings from the work of SDSN and explores the idea of applying systems thinking to approaching the SDGs in higher education.

Other existing global networks of universities have explicitly adopted the SDGs and are creating spaces of collaboration. As another chapter in this volume describes, one of the oldest and largest higher education associations in the world, the Association of Commonwealth Universities (ACU) – a community of 500 universities across 50 countries – has adopted global sustainable development as one of its top priorities and has established several collaborative programs to support its members and leverage their combined resources.

Our own university, Georgia Tech, helped found the University Global Coalition with a group of like-minded institutions and the United Nations Institute for Training and Research (UNITAR) around a set of six commitments in support of the SDGs. The coalition organizes events and conferences, facilitates the exchange of best practices, facilitates dialogue among university leaders, and supports members in forming partnerships around SDG-focused initiatives. In this book, we highlight several other examples of networks and draw lessons that will hopefully inspire others.

While a growing number of institutions have adopted strategies in support of the SDGs, many have been either slow to adopt or outright sceptical that the SDGs are achievable or that universities can make a difference. Those who have undertaken a Voluntary University Review (VUR) of progress along the 17 goals (Alaoui, 2021) or reported to The Times Higher Education Impact Ratings – which assess SDG actions across research, stewardship, outreach, and teaching – have found just how difficult it is to classify and inventory work under each goal, capture the extent of their university's engagement with the goals, and, perhaps most importantly, accelerate commitments and actions (Times Higher Education, 2022). It is impractical to expect institutions to have equal impact on all goals; we, as institutions, have intentionally developed areas of expertise and impact based on years of building resources and strategy.

And yet, it is essential that we accelerate universities' engagement. Higher education complements the unique capabilities of government, business, and non-profit organizations, and brings resources no one else can. Partnerships can be effective vehicles to inspire and sustain action, connect complementary capabilities, and exchange best practices.

A guide published by SDSN, *Accelerating Education for the SDGs in Universities* (2020), argues that 'university programs around sustainable development are best organized according to the problems they seek to address'. This guide recommends a combination of creating new organizational units in sustainable development, new educational programs, incentives for high-level policy advising and analysis work by faculty and students, and seeking out international partnerships to amplify sustainable development work.

The partnerships discussed in this volume are diverse in scope and goals, yet they collectively show a few patterns or principles that may be useful to others. Our own experiences and our analysis of others lead to some recommendations around four steps: Plan, Evaluate, Prioritize, and Partner.

PLAN

Any engagement in a sustainable development partnership starts by clarifying the why, evaluating one's own strengths and capabilities, identifying the areas of greatest need, and defining success. There is a difference between an iterative process and a scope with no boundaries, and the latter runs the risk to burn out people and resources without producing meaningful results.

While visible support from executive leadership is key to ensure an interdisciplinary approach, it is not sufficient; critical stakeholders in academics, research, operations, and community must be engaged from initiation to ensure a university-wide effort.

The work of sustainable development is very broad, and not all universities can do all things. Two basic project management tools could be helpful: (1) a project charter – including scope, timeline with milestones and responsible parties, definition of deliverables, and at least one executive sponsor who can consult with university leaders and make decisions on behalf of the entire university; and (2) a stakeholder engagement plan – who should be engaged and how, what is their level of influence, the impact this work will have on them, and their support for the efforts.

Resourcing discussions are a key part of this planning process. In lessons learned from our peers who have completed university-wide SDG reporting, undertaking this process without dedicated staff or faculty time is next to impossible. Ideally, the staff and faculty who comprise the project team will be temporarily relieved of a portion of their responsibilities to focus extensively on this effort, will have the support of student researchers, and will have a strong knowledge of institutional workings and resources. This is not work that can be easily contracted out.

EVALUATE

This initial assessment should provide a robust platform to frame the data-gathering stage about existing capabilities and programs, strengths and weaknesses, and areas of opportunity. The VUR may offer a useful framework to assess a university's impact on all 17 goals. The idea is to evaluate existing research and educational programs, operational performance and alignment, and partnerships towards each of the goals. The VUR should include a review of research publications through the university, existing coursework, external and intramural funding, and ongoing collaborations for each goal.

The VUR provides an opportunity to engage the broader campus community, which helps bring awareness on the goals and increase commitment, while gathering data. It can help expose connections among different departments working on similar or related topics through different disciplinary lenses as well as linkages among goals. It can be a source of new ideas for partnerships, provide general education on the SDGs for the campus community, and a comprehensive data set that can be shared with potential partners.

VURs can range from static reports to dynamic formats where information can be continuously updated to include new efforts and partnerships and allow the campus community to interact with the data.

An intermediate step, short of a comprehensive VUR, might be an evaluation of research publications based on the SDGs. Programs, such as the SDG Research Mapping Initiative from Elsevier, the Times Higher Education SDG rankings data partner, can help scan and tag publications with the goals to provide an initial analysis (Elsevier, *SDG Research*). A complementary activity, that can be undertaken as part of a VUR or separately, is the 17 Rooms process, described by its co-creators at the Brookings Institution and The Rockefeller Foundation as 'an experimental method for advancing the economic, social, and environmental priorities embedded in the world's Sustainable Development Goals (SDGs)'. 17 Rooms brings transdisciplinary teams together in 17 working groups, or 'Rooms', representing each of the 17 SDGs. Throughout the process, each group collaborates to identify partnership actions that can advance each SDG over the next 12–18 months (Brookings, *17 Rooms*).

PRIORITIZE

While faculty champions throughout the university will inevitably pursue a range of self-organized projects and initiatives, declaring institutional priorities can help align efforts, attract external investment, amplify impact, and provide a framework for analyzing potential partners and partnerships. Ideally, priorities should emerge at the intersection of institutional strengths and community needs.

The institution's strategic plan and the VUR (or whatever assessment is available) are great sources to identify strengths. At our own institution, the strategic planning process engaged more than 5,000 individuals and has a great deal of community ownership. Priorities linked to it enjoy a stronger sense of legitimacy and acceptance.

In terms of needs, tools such as the Voluntary Local Review, discussions with local leaders, and data from local non-profits focused on community betterment and empowerment can provide critical inputs. A combination of the strengths and needs assessment can help us narrow a long list down to a handful of strategic priorities in sustainable development.

The most important outcome of this stage is a deeper understanding of the alignment between institutional strengths and specific SDGs, as well as the weaknesses or missing assets necessary to find and implement effective solutions.

PARTNER

Partnerships require both awareness of and confidence in one's strengths as well as humility in appreciating one's limitations. This is particularly important in the context of the extraordinarily complex, multistakeholder, and multidisciplinary problems articulated by the SDGs.

An effective partnership is built on a shared sense of purpose, the recognition of one's blind spots, and the belief that bringing diverse perspectives and assets are essential to find better solutions. The partnership endures through mutual trust and support, sharing of information and rewards, and fair conflict resolution (Butcher et al., 2011).

Given the importance of partnerships in achieving the SDGs, the UN is providing resources to train and guide the establishment of effective partnerships. Programs like the Partnership Accelerator and the Partnering Initiative offer training and advisory services to member states and UN entities engaged in forming partnerships. One particularly valuable resource, the *SDG Partnership Guidebook,* provides a valuable starting point in moving from a simple exchange of resources to working towards system change, what they refer to as 'transformational partnerships'. It includes a series of planning and evaluative tools, a definition of strengths, roles, and expectations of different sectors in SDG partnerships, and guidance on the partnership process (Stibbe & Prescott, 2020).

Partnership formation is not a linear process. There is constant need for discussion, reevaluation, and sometimes, redirection. A written agreement developed by and agreed to by all partners at the onset of partnership can provide a foundation and understanding of project elements that often cause partnerships to fail – definition of purpose and shared beliefs, definition of roles, expected benefits for all partners, agreed upon metrics of both effort and impact, and a shared definition of success.

A PREVIEW OF WHAT'S AHEAD

In evaluating various higher education partnerships devoted to sustainable development, it becomes clear that there are no formulaic approaches that will work for all universities. While our missions share much, our geographic and social environments, our historical circumstances, our governance, size and structure, create a very different landscape for each institution – different strengths and opportunities, and different types of potential partners and partnerships.

In this volume we have sought out a wide variety of partnerships with the hope that elements from each of them may inspire action elsewhere and provide valuable insights. Each chapter's authors explore a unique set of partnerships either within higher education or across other sectors. Authors take a critical perspective of where higher education's approach to the SDGs is lacking, highlight lessons learned and specific examples of effective partnerships, and explore how we can increase impact.

Nikhil Seth, who leads the UNITAR, sets the stage describing higher education's role in the formation of the goals and sharing a vision for the role higher education can play in the future. He notes the unique convening abilities of higher education in bringing together community voices across sectors.

Tahl S. Kestin, Julio Lumbreras, and María Cortés Puch use their experience with the SDSN to propose a systems approach to drive change in higher education in support of the SDGs. Their chapter details some of the barriers that exist within higher education institutions including culture, resources, incentives, institutional processes and silos, and external factors, such as political, social, cultural, and economic contexts. From here they explore the concept of a systems approach and propose an adaptive leadership model to align universities with the SDGs.

In a chapter exploring the power of inter-university SDG networks, Joanna Newman of the ACU provides examples of how ACU has utilized their extensive global network for collective action. She details how networks can help decrease the barriers of systemic bias for universities in low- to middle-income countries through programs such as peer research networks, development of blended learning courses, and topical networks within networks to advance research, learning, and best practices on pressing global issues such as climate change.

From an exploration of the power of systems thinking and networks to effect large-scale change, we move into case studies of how universities can partner for impact. Susan T. L. Harrison and Maano Ramutsindela of University of Cape Town explore how community, government, and industry partnerships can advance regional and national impact and give the primary voice to communities that have often been an afterthought in decisions that affect them greatly. They share how examples, such as the work of the African chapter of the IPCC, of a program focused on community-based interventions in cancer, of the development of a transdisciplinary program in mining science and policy, and of rapid responses to COVID-19, can centre the voice and knowledge of the Global South in solutions building.

A chapter about the Millennium Campus Network illustrates how partnerships may be initiated by students themselves. Sam Vaghar, Summer Wyatt-Buchan, Shriya Dayal, Srijan Banik, and Ayushi Nahar provide a vision for empowering student leaders and testimony from several Millennium Fellows projects. Sam Vaghar describes the impetus, founding, challenges, and successes in building the Millennium Campus Network and how their inclusive approach to partnerships helped create the Millennium Fellowship. His co-authors, all former Millennium Fellows, share their projects in building bridges and personal relationships with refugees, menstrual health, climate education, building an education hub, and developing a program to build financial literacy and independence for women. Through their projects and key reflections, they emphasize the importance of trusting, empowering, and incentivizing students while giving them tools to support growth.

With a focus on teaching partnerships, Luz Patricia Montaño-Salinas and José Manuel Páez-Borrallo of the Instituto Tecnológico de Monterrey share the story of their innovative global virtual exchange program and the power of connecting students and instructors with different perspectives and from different geographies to address a common challenge. They share the pre-Covid beginnings of the virtual exchange program and the impetus during Covid to quickly expand virtual course offerings, to date reaching over 15,000 students. Their story illustrates the importance of explicit institutional commitment, with Tecnológico de Monterrey's commitment to the SDGs as an example.

Our volume closes with a focus on university–business partnerships based on the work of colleagues from our own institution. Marilyn Brown (Georgia Institute of Technology), Jasmine Crowe (Goodr), John A. Lanier (Ray C. Anderson Foundation), Michael Oxman (Georgia Tech), Roy Richards, Jr (Southwire Company), and L. Beril Toktay (Georgia Tech) introduce the Drawdown Georgia Business Compact, a science-based collaboration between higher education, business, and the philanthropic sector to advance climate action in Georgia. The authors share the backstory of Drawdown Georgia and the process of developing the Business Compact and engaging the business community to make research-based commitments to climate action.

A CALL TO COLLABORATE

Most institutions are programed to work in competitive environments. Universities are no exception. We compete for financial resources (government appropriations, private donations, and research contracts), human resources (students, faculty, and staff), and public recognition (rankings, peer approval, and prestige). The implicit assumption is that resources are limited and scarce and our role is to claim our share in a zero-sum game. The expectation is that the sum-total of competition will bring about benefits for all.

The idea behind the SDGs is that the resources to find solutions to our most pressing challenges are abundant yet disconnected and misaligned, and that institutional self-interest will not be sufficient to tackle these challenges. This belief was explicitly articulated into SDG17. Unlike the other 16 goals, SDG17 does not address what needs to be solved but how. It calls for collaboration across sectors, countries, and disciplines. It calls for alignment of objectives and connection of disparate resources and capabilities in pursuing those objectives.

Universities are essential pieces of the global puzzle needed to achieve the SDGs, and partnerships will be central to their ability to contribute their share. Effective partnering does not mean to leave aside our culture of competition, but it does require that we acknowledge it and work with it. Effective partnering starts by bringing clarity to one's own purpose and goals, to one's own definition of success, and to one's strengths and weaknesses. Effective partnering requires also reflecting on one's local and global context, prioritizing, deciding on what matters, and accepting that we depend on others and assume the vulnerability of relying on others. Effective partnering is ultimately built on the belief that we can get further and achieve more with others than we can on our own.

The stakes are high. The problems have been defined. And universities have been called to action. It is time that we respond.

REFERENCES

Alaoui, S. (2021, August 12). 7 *Innovative ways American Universities are driving progress on the SDGs*. United Nations Foundation. https://unfoundation.org/blog/post/7-innovative-ways-american-universities-are-driving-progress-on-the-sdgs/

Butcher, J., Bezzina, M., & Moran, W. (2011). Transformational partnerships: A new agenda for higher education. *Innovative Higher Education*, *36*, 29–40. http://doi.org/10.1007/s10755-010-9155-7.

Elsevier. *SDG* research mapping initiative. https://www.elsevier.com/about/partnerships/sdg-research-mapping-initiative

International Monetary Fund. (2022). *World inequality report*. https://wir2022.wid.world/

National Science Foundation (2022). Rankings by total R&D expenditures. https://ncsesdata.nsf.gov/profiles/site?method=rankingbysource&ds=herd

Sawhill, J., & Williamson, D. (2001, May 1). *Measuring what matters in nonprofits*. McKinsey Quarterly. https://www.mckinsey.com/industries/public-and-social-sector/our-insights/measuring-what-matters-in-nonprofits

SDSN. (2020). *Accelerating education for the SDGs in universities: A guide for universities, colleges, and tertiary and higher education institutions*. Sustainable Development Solutions Network (SDSN).

Stibbe, D., & Prescott, D. (2020). *The SDG partnership guidebook: A practical guide to building high-impact multi-stakeholder partnerships for the sustainable development goals*. The Partnering Initiative and UNDESA.

The Brookings Institution. *17 Rooms*. https://www.brookings.edu/project/17-rooms/

The World Bank. (2022). *School enrollment, tertiary (% Gross)*. UNESCO Institute for Statistics Data. https://data.worldbank.org/indicator/SE.TER.ENRR

Times Higher Education. (2022, April 27). *THE impact rankings 2022 released*. https://www.timeshighereducation.com/press-releases/impact-rankings-2022-released

UN Sustainable Development Solutions Network. *About us*. https://www.unsdsn.org/about-us

Unruh, G. C. (2000). Understanding carbon lock-in. *Energy Policy*, *28*(12), 817–830. https://www.sciencedirect.com/science/article/abs/pii/S0301421500000707

World Economic Forum. (2022, September 12). *This is how much the global literacy rate grew over 200 years*. https://www.weforum.org/agenda/2022/09/reading-writing-global-literacy-rate-changed/

2

SDG 17 AND THE ROLE OF UNIVERSITIES ACHIEVING AGENDA 2030

Nikhil Seth

ABSTRACT

The profound impacts of the COVID-19 pandemic are being exacerbated by political, economic, social, and environmental crisis and have set back almost all Sustainable Development Goals (SDGs). In order to re-focus our energy to make progress according to the SDGs, education, research, innovation, and leadership will be essential in helping societies address the challenges outlined in Agenda 2030 and the SDGs. Universities, with their broad remit around the creation and dissemination of knowledge and their unique position within society, have a critical role to play in the achievement of the SDGs. Arguably none of the SDGs will be achieved without this sector. Engaging with the SDGs can also benefit universities by helping to demonstrate university impact, capture demand for SDG-related education, build new partnerships, access new funding streams, and define a university that is responsible and globally aware. This chapter's thesis is that the SDGs will not be achieved without the strategic engagement by the academic sector and that aligning a university's learning and teaching goals, research, and operational incentives with the SDGs can provide new opportunities and business models. The author will also provide background on higher education's role in the formation of the SDGs and how this process has framed higher education's role in achieving the SDGs.

Keywords: Agenda 2030; Sustainable Development Goals; SDG history; leadership; higher education; United Nations

As we are now less than a decade away from 2030, it is more urgent than ever to accelerate how higher education institutions (HEI) take leadership in supporting the necessary transformations towards achieving the SDGs and implementing the 2030 Agenda. As a first step, this chapter is focused on analysing the critical role academia in general and HEIs had in developing the SDGs. This is followed by highlighting how HEIs support achieving the SDGs both internally, through education, research, and campus practices, as well as by contributing to policy-making at all levels in society. Today's complex and multiple challenges – the COVID-19 pandemic, climate crisis, inequality, wars – are a threat for the SDGs. But they offer an opportunity for renewed multilateral action and search for new innovative solutions that change the status quo and old ways of doing things, including for HEIs.

Let us first take a step back and reflect on the 2030 Agenda and the SDGs. What is so special about this Agenda? After all, the United Nations (UN) has adopted so many declarations, agendas, and platforms for action over 75 years of existence. Why will the SDGs endure? To answer this question, I turn for inspiration to the UN Charter, which enshrines the hopes of humanity for peace and prosperity. It is inspirational, and, after so many years, it is the 'bible' of multilateralism. In the same vein, I often feel that the 2030 Agenda is a transformation of the Charter into a plan with goals, targets, and indicators. The 2030 Agenda was created as the result of an awe-inspiring journey with unprecedented participation and ownership. When it was adopted, there was applause from every part of the UN General Assembly Hall – from governments of all different political hues and on different rungs of the development ladder, from the UN System, from academia, business, and civil society. The Agenda has broken the North–South way of looking at issues and instead embraced the future of our common humanity through the principle of universality. It has made sustainable development to the business of everyone and has given a fresh flavour to the meaning of global citizenship. What were the ingredients that brought us the 2030 Agenda? The following focuses on the multiple stakeholders with a specific view of the role of academia during the process of developing the SDGs.

While the SDGs were developed by an Open Working Group (OWG) of UN member states, all stakeholders, including civil society, academia, the private sector, and of course the UN System, were brought into the negotiations. The door was cracked open in Rio de Janeiro at the Earth Summit in 1992. Yet by 2012, it was not a question of civil society 'observing' negotiations but participating in a meaningful way. There is always pushback to this openness, and the OWG was no exception. The chairs of the OWG, guided by the Secretariat, provided suitable windows for the participation of the non-governmental entities. The Secretariat took the extra step of providing briefings every morning, explaining the day's activities and negotiations, urging different interests to align with the day's discussion rather than focusing only on their specific interest. This organised participation helped facilitate more meaningful engagement and provided greater space, and ultimately, greater ownership of the final outcome.

Academia, in general, and institutions of higher learning engaged in the process which created the SDGs. Decisions in the UN are taken by member states, but making intelligent decisions is strongly guided by inputs, including from academic experts. This took many forms in the SDG process. The SDG team in the UN Secretariat combed academic literature in preparing for the session of the OWG to identify academic authorities to speak on topics for the agenda: The Nobel laureate Abijit Banerjee of MIT spoke on poverty eradication; Sabine Alkire of Oxford University spoke about the multidimensional poverty index; Larry Summers' work provided some ideas on reducing inequalities; Joe Stiglitz, Jeffrey Sachs, and the Science and Technology Community also helped in briefing the members states. These briefings added great value to the texts we prepared for the governments to negotiate.

THE ROLE HEI CAN PLAY IN ACHIEVING THE SDGS

Education and research are explicitly recognised in a number of the SDGs, and universities have a direct role in addressing these. However, the contribution of universities to the SDGs is much broader, as they can support the implementation of every one of the SDGs as well as the implementation of the SDG framework itself.

Education is one of the bedrocks of the SDGs. In and of itself, quality education leads to significant sustainable development benefits for individuals, communities, and countries. It is also a critical means of supporting and accelerating global capacity to implement the SDGs. As such, universities, through their extensive learning and teaching activities – including undergraduate and graduate teaching, professional training, executive and adult education, online learning, co-curricular activities, and student clubs and societies – have a very important role to play in SDG implementation, by providing students with the knowledge, skills, and motivation to understand and address the SDGs (broadly 'education for sustainable development'); providing in-depth academic or vocational expertise to implement SDG solutions; providing accessible, affordable, and inclusive education to all; providing capacity building for students and professionals from developing countries; and empowering and mobilising young people.

Further, to achieve the SDGs, the global community needs to overcome many difficult and complex social, economic, and environmental challenges, some of which require transformations in how societies and economies function and how we interact with our planet. Universities, through their *extensive research capabilities and activities*, have a critical role in providing the necessary knowledge, evidence-base, solutions, and innovations to underpin and support the implementation of the SDGs by the global community – through both traditional disciplinary approaches and newer interdisciplinary, transdisciplinary, and sustainability science approaches; providing capacity building for developing countries in undertaking and using research; collaborating with and supporting innovative companies to implement SDG solutions; improving diversity in research; and student training for sustainable development research.

Third, universities and HEIs are often large entities and can have significant impacts on the social, cultural, and environmental well-being within their campuses, communities, and regions – and sometimes far beyond. These impacts directly relate to all areas of the SDGs, and *by acting responsibly* universities can make significant contributions to their achievement. All organisations have some impact on how the SDGs are manifested within their operational sphere of influence. Depending on the nature and size of the organisation, its impacts on some – and sometimes all – of the SDGs can be significant. By identifying these impacts and acting responsibly to address them, all HEIs can contribute to the SDGs. Universities are often major employers, consumers, investors, and owners of real estate. They oversee large communities of staff, students, and contractors. Their campuses can function like and be the size of small cities. They can create significant flows of people and goods that necessitate infrastructure investment in surrounding areas. They can also have an influence far beyond their regions through their supply chains and increasingly international reach. As a result, universities have an impact across each and every one of the SDGs, and this impact can be large. By implementing the principles of the SDGs through governance structures and operational policies and decisions, such as those relating to employment, finance, campus services, support services, facilities, procurement, human resources, and student administration, HEIs can have a big impact.

The scale of the task of achieving the SDGs requires *mobilisation of all sectors*. As the UN's Transforming our World document states:

> *The future of humanity and of our planet lies in our hands … We have mapped the road to sustainable development; it will be for all of us to ensure that the journey is successful and its gains irreversible. (United Nations, 2015)*

The journey

> *will involve Governments as well as parliaments, the UN system and other international institutions, local authorities, indigenous peoples, civil society, business and the private sector, the scientific and academic community – and all people.*

Collaboration is crucial, as encapsulated in target 17.16 to

> *Enhance the Global Partnership for Sustainable Development, complemented by multi-stakeholder partnerships that mobilize and share knowledge, expertise, technology and financial resources, to support the achievement of the Sustainable Development Goals in all countries ....*

Mobilisation and collaboration on this scale needs significant leadership and support to bring all stakeholders on board, build their capacity to understand and implement the SDGs, and facilitate conversations, mutual learning, and partnerships between different sectors. The public itself is a key stakeholder in SDG implementation in identifying the priorities, debating the options, and contributing to implementation in their own lives. In most countries the public has little knowledge of the SDGs and little opportunity to actively participate in implementation. As places devoted to knowledge creation and teaching for the benefit of society, universities have traditionally occupied a unique position in society that makes them particularly suited to provide leadership on SDG implementation. They are trusted by the public and are seen as neutral actors by other sectors. Many have significant prominence and influence in the public sphere. And they have expertise in research and education that is essential for building capacity and supporting policy-making. While many universities have struggled to maintain this critical role under 'rationalisation and commercialisation' processes, the SDGs provide an opportunity to enhance this role.

Universities have another crucial role – backstopping policy at the national level and providing policy support to organisations and institutions. In many countries there is a seamless exchange between academia and governments. The ability to mainstream SDG learning in policy is the essential task of individual experts. Helping shift policy-making and budget formulation from the typical silos and historical inertia is very urgent. The cross-fertilisation of ideas, the adoption of new tools, data, and analysis is vital for change. It is my hope that this exchange will become the norm rather than a rare exception.

I wish to see the same energy of academia and the institutions of higher education, demonstrated in the creation of the SDGs and in the early part of its implementation, to continue as we head towards 2030 and dream of the world we want and deserve.

REFERENCE

United Nations. (2015). Transforming our world: The 2030 agenda for sustainable development. https://sdgs.un.org/2030agenda

3

MOBILIZING HIGHER EDUCATION ACTION ON THE SDGs: INSIGHTS FROM SYSTEM CHANGE APPROACHES

Tahl S. Kestin, Julio Lumbreras and María Cortés Puch

ABSTRACT

Higher education institutions (HEIs) are increasingly recognizing that their unique functions and expertise in research, education, and community leadership make them essential societal partners for helping achieve the Sustainable Development Goals (SDGs). However, the sector is not reaching its full potential, or acting fast enough, given the dire state of global progress on the SDGs. There has been a growing recognition that higher education's (HE) ability to scale up action on the SDGs is hampered by a range of systemic and structural barriers within institutions, the HE sector, and the local and global contexts more broadly. However, many of these barriers and the potential solutions for overcoming them have been known for years, and a key challenge HE now faces is how to put these changes into practice. In this chapter, we build on insights from the work of the Sustainable Development Solutions Network

(SDSN) and others on system transformations for sustainable development, as well as our own work on HE engagement with the SDGs, to propose several 'meta' reasons that might be hampering efforts to scale up HE action on the SDGs, as well as some suggested approaches for addressing them. These approaches include treating HE as a system, defining better the outcomes we are aiming for, employing adaptive leadership approaches, and investing in genuine partnerships. While a detailed treatment of these approaches is beyond the scope of this chapter, we hope to encourage the HE community to look at this old problem in new ways.

Keywords: Sustainable development goals; higher education; transformations; systems change; barriers; levers

1. INTRODUCTION

The SDSN was created 10 years ago to 'mobilize the world's universities and knowledge institutions to play their historic role in the great transformation to sustainable development' that is being guided by the SDGs (Sachs & Thwaites, 2022).

SDSN now works with over 1,700 member institutions, 50 regional and country networks, and hundreds of partners from governments, business, civil society, youth, and UN agencies and other international organizations, to develop integrated solutions and pathways for a wide range of sustainable development challenges.

A key aspect of mobilizing SDSN's membership has been to understand the barriers for HEIs to scale up their contributions to the SDGs and to support HEIs to overcome them. Over recent years we have engaged with hundreds of HEIs all over the world, through initiatives such as the preparation of sector guides (SDSN, 2020; SDSN Australia/Pacific, 2017), five years of convening dedicated conference tracks as part of the International Conference on Sustainable Development, the development of case study repositories (e.g. blogs.upm.es/education4sdg), hosting of global and regional meetings with university presidents (SDSN Secretariat, 2022), and facilitation of communities of practice and discussions among SDSN member institutions (e.g. the *Accelerating SDG Practice Initiative* of SDSN Australia, New Zealand & Pacific).

Reflecting on this engagement work, as well as on the SDSN's and our own institutions' more general work on system transformations for sustainable development, we have come to believe that the systems change lens is essential for understanding and overcoming barriers to HE SDG action.

In this chapter, we put forward the rationale behind this thinking, as well as some insights this gives rise to, and approaches for overcoming these barriers (Section 4). To set the scene, Section 2 recaps the case for why HE needs to scale up its action on the SDGs, and Section 3 provides an overview of the barriers and why they are proving so hard to overcome.

2. THE CASE FOR SCALING UP HE ACTION ON THE SDGs

The world is approaching the midway point for achieving the 2030 Agenda and the SDGs. However, progress on the SDGs, already inadequate before the pandemic, is now in even greater jeopardy as a result of the pandemic and multiple other global and local crises (Sachs et al., 2022; United Nations, 2022).

Despite these setbacks, Sachs et al. (2022) have called on the world to not only stay the course on the SDGs, but also to redouble our efforts to achieve them by promoting six transformations (Sachs et al., 2019):

1. Quality education (SDG 4)
2. Access to good quality and affordable health care (SDG 3)
3. Renewable energy and a circular economy (SDGs 7, 12, and 13)
4. Sustainable land and marine management (SDGs 2, 14, and 15)
5. Sustainable urban infrastructure (SDGs 6, 9, and 11)
6. Universal access to digital services (SDG 9)

All of these SDG transformations need strong and urgent contributions from science and academia. As we discussed in SDSN

Australia/Pacific (2017) and SDSN (2020), examples of how HEIs can contribute to this agenda include:

- *Learning and teaching*: Providing students with the knowledge, skills, and motivation to understand and address the SDGs (broadly 'education for the SDGs'); providing in-depth academic or vocational expertise to implement SDG solutions; providing accessible, affordable, and inclusive education to all; providing capacity building for students and professionals from developing countries; and empowering and mobilizing young people.
- *Research*: Providing the necessary knowledge, evidence-base, solutions, technologies, pathways, and innovations to underpin and support the implementation of the SDGs by the global community – through both traditional disciplinary approaches and newer interdisciplinary, transdisciplinary, and sustainability science approaches; providing capacity building for developing countries in undertaking and using research; collaborating with and supporting innovative companies to implement SDG solutions; improving diversity in research; and student training for sustainable development research.
- *Community leadership*: Strengthening public engagement and participation in addressing the SDGs; initiating and facilitating cross-sectoral dialogue and action; ensuring HE sector representation in national implementation; helping to design SDG-based policies; and demonstrating sector commitment to the SDGs.

Conversely, lack of action by HEIs in these areas is at best a missed opportunity to drive progress, and at worst can lead to lock-in of inappropriate practices, as every student who graduates without the knowledge and skills to address climate change and sustainable development in their profession may contribute to perpetuating unsustainable practices.

On the surface, HEIs have recognized and embraced the SDGs and sustainability as a focus for institutional action. The SDSN now has over 1,700 member universities and knowledge institutions; the 2022 Times Higher Education Impact Rankings had over 1,400 participants (Ellis et al., 2022); and hundreds of HEIs have signed various HE commitments to the SDGs and climate change, such as the SDG Accord, the University Commitment to the SDGs, the University Global Coalition Agreement, and Race to Zero.

However, the degree of engagement within HE has been too little and too slow given the urgency of the challenges the world faces (UNESCO, 2022), leading to growing calls, including our own, for HE to scale up its engagement with and contributions to the SDGs (e.g. Giesenbauer & Müller-Christ, 2020; Purcell & Haddock-Fraser, 2023; SDSN, 2020; UNESCO, 2022).

Why has it been so difficult for HE to respond fully to the SDGs? How can we overcome these difficulties? In the next section, we explore some of the barriers to SDG action, as well as some of the solutions that have been put forward, to suggest some initial reasons why addressing them is so difficult.

3. BARRIERS TO SDG ACTION

The SDGs require institutions and individuals to do new things in new ways, and this change is associated with a range of systemic and structural barriers within individual institutions, the HE sector, and the local and global contexts more broadly (e.g. Care et al., 2021; Leal Filho et al., 2017; SDSN, 2020; UNESCO, 2022). Identifying these barriers is an important first step in finding ways to address them and eventually making the necessary structural changes to transition into an environment where HE responds fully to the SDGs.

In this section, we provide a brief overview of some of the common personal, organizational, and external barriers hampering HEIs from scaling up action on the SDGs, using SDSN (2020) as a starting point (Section 3.1). We then evaluate this list in terms of potential approaches for addressing or overcoming these barriers, and their potential for success (Section 3.2).

3.1. Common Barriers to SDG Action

3.1.1. Personal Barriers

Expanding and deepening action on the SDGs in HEIs requires the support and cooperation of a wide range of individuals within the institution, including institutional leadership, academic and professional staff, and students. However, these stakeholders may not be interested or able to have a greater focus on addressing the SDGs for reasons such as:

- Mindsets that are resistant to change or to letting go of aspects of one's work, do not see the benefit or relevance of the SDGs to their work, or are sceptical of the value of the SDG agenda.
- Lack of capacity, time, or funding for new endeavours; lack of relevant knowledge on the SDGs or the skills to implement the SDGs in their work; lack of access to appropriate support and resources; lack of incentives; and competing priorities.
- Incentives that reward actions less compatible with the needs of addressing the SDGs, such as narrow disciplinary focus or solitary work over partnerships.

3.1.2. Organizational Barriers

Institutional structures, policies, and processes, and lack of leadership, capacity, and resources, can limit or slow down HEIs' ability to play a relevant role in implementing the SDGs. Some of the main organizational barriers and challenges include:

- Barriers to institutional change, such as rigidity in processes, slowness in adaptation processes, lack of alignment between faculty and administrations, outdated hierarchical structures, lack of innovative vision, misaligned incentives, resistant cultural norms, and lack of leadership (top-down and bottom-up).
- Silos that hinder collaboration across disciplines or institutional areas (e.g. learning & teaching, research, operations, and student clubs and societies).
- Lack of institutional capacities and resources to implement cross-institutional change, including financial resources, human resources, technical capacities, and knowledge and expertise across all areas of the SDGs.

3.1.3. External Barriers

HEIs operate within a complex external context that may not be aligned with the required changes needed to implement the SDGs, which thus hinders or discourages HEIs from taking action. This includes:

- The institutional environment, the multilayered set of rules and requirements to which universities must conform in order to receive legitimacy, resources, and support, can fail to encourage, or might actively discourage, universities from implementing the SDGs. This environment involves a diversity of official and non-official mechanisms and actors, such as legislation, funding and contracting schemes, quality assurance frameworks, official or voluntary accreditation processes, professional or disciplinary accreditation bodies, and rankings.
- Social, cultural, political, and economic contexts can influence what agenda universities feel they are able to pursue and invest in. While the SDGs have been adopted by all 193 UN member nations, priorities and support for different aspects of the agenda can vary locally or among different groups. Market forces and the economic situation can also significantly affect what universities can do.

3.2. Potential Solutions

Approaches for overcoming some of the barriers described in Section 3.1 have been suggested recently by, for example, SDSN (2020) and UNESCO (2022). They include actions such as building capacity and skills of staff; changing incentives structures; providing funding and time for change; changing academic culture; ensuring high-level support; expanding cross-institution, interdisciplinary, and cross-sector collaborations and partnerships; sharing resources between institutions; and advocating for changes in national funding structures or accreditation requirements.

However, as we noted in SDSN (2020), while these solutions might work on a small scale, implementing them across institutions or across the sector is likely to be difficult, or slow, because they are incompatible within the traditional structure of HEIs. In addition, we reflect on the fact that some of these barriers and potential solutions have been recognized for many years – for example, as reviewed by Leal Filho et al. (2017). It therefore appears the real challenge we are facing is not so much working out what needs to change, but rather how to put solutions into practice.

In SDSN (2020) we also proposed a more innovative approach – the implementation of a 'second operating system' – to put some of these solutions into practice.

Based on a concept proposed by Kotter (2012), the second operating system starts as a smaller unit within an institution (such as a dedicated institute or a network) that is set up to pursue new ways of engaging with the SDGs. This allows the 'first operating system' – the existing governing system – to continue to deliver high quality work and ongoing commitments. The second operating system can also be used as a living lab to trial approaches to overcoming internal HE barriers to transformation – such as how to break academic silos, different incentive schemes, etc.

However, even this solution may not be able to translate to the scale of change required. In large institutions, the second operating system risks not permeating sufficiently into the rest of the organization, and therefore its transformative capacity might be limited to a 'bubble' within the organization.

This may happen if there isn't a strong commitment from the leadership to begin with, if the second operating system isn't sufficiently representative of the whole system, or if the second operating system challenges the first system in a way that is not accepted by people in power.

For the reasons above, we are trying in this chapter to think bigger about how to overcome the barriers to HE SDG action. In the next section, we explore some of the factors that are hindering this from happening and potential approaches for how we can start thinking about this old problem in new ways.

4. 'META' APPROACHES TO MOBILIZING SDG ACTION

The barriers and challenges to scaling up HE action on the SDGs that were discussed in Section 3 have been known for a while.

Why have they been so difficult to overcome? In this section, we take a step back and explore some potential 'meta' reasons that might be hampering our ability to address these more specific barriers and challenges, as well as some approaches for overcoming them.

In particular, we have turned for inspiration and lessons learned to the work that the SDSN and our own institutions (the Monash Sustainable Development Institute and the Universidad Politécnica de Madrid's Centro de Innovación en Tecnología para el Desarrollo Humano) have been doing to drive large-scale transformations for sustainable development across a range of contexts. Examples of some of these initiatives include:

- *The World in 2050* (TWI2050 – The World in 2050, 2018), which is developing pathways to try to simultaneously achieve all the 17 SDGs, using integrative and systemic methodological approaches.
- *The Food, Agriculture, Biodiversity, Land-Use and Energy (FABLE) Consortium* (FABLE, 2020), which is developing national-scale food and land-use strategies aligned with global climate and sustainability goals, to foster problem-solving and iterative learning.
- *The Climateworks Centre* (Browett & Denis-Ryan, 2021), which is focusing on aligning emissions reductions across seven physical and enabling systems of the economy with a trajectory that limits global warming to 1.5°C.
- *The EU Cities Mission* (European Commission Directorate-General for Research & Innovation, 2020, 2021) aims to transform 100 cities towards climate neutrality and to contribute to public policies and the 2030 Agenda through collaborations (multiactor partnerships) operating in the medium and long term. The Mission is being implemented through the NetZeroCities platform (netzerocities.eu).

As the SDGs and most systems in our world are connected, transformation for sustainability requires a holistic perspective (TWI2050 – The World in 2050, 2018). The core approach used by these initiatives is systems change, which aims to transform systems that, among other things, have multiple and highly interlinked components and actors, as well as diverse and competing priorities (Grin et al., 2010; Horan, 2019). Some of the important elements of this approach (OECD & SDSN, 2019) include:

- A deep mapping and understanding of how the system works and its drivers.
- A definition of the desired outcomes and clear and measurable targets.
- Working backwards from the target to develop potential pathways to achieve the target.
- Engaging all stakeholders connected to the system on defining the targets and assessing the pathways, including potential tradeoffs.

If this sustainable development transformation approach can be applied to such a diverse range of contexts, can it help address – or at least understand better – the challenges of HE transformations for the SDGs?

While a full-blown implementation of such an approach in HE is beyond the scope of this chapter, we believe that applying this lens can provide insights into the 'meta' reasons that have made addressing the barriers discussed in Section 3.1 so challenging, as well as suggest potential approaches for overcoming them. In particular, in Sections 4.1–4.4 we briefly explore the following four ideas:

- Treating HE as a system
- Defining better the outcomes we are aiming for
- Employing adaptive leadership approaches
- Investing in building genuine partnerships

4.1. Treating HE as a System

The barriers to greater contributions by HE to the SDGs that we described in Section 3 mostly relate to discrete functions or components of

HEIs or the sector more broadly. Solutions typically focus on changing these discrete functions or components. However, HE is in fact a complex, interconnected and dynamic system, and addressing these barriers therefore requires a systems change approach.

Fig. 3.1 offers one way of conceptualizing a HE institution as a system with different sectors. While each institution will look a bit different, depending on factors such as its size, context, and areas of focus, Fig. 3.1 captures some of the complexity and interconnections within the institution, as well as some of the influences of a wide range of external drivers and stakeholders.

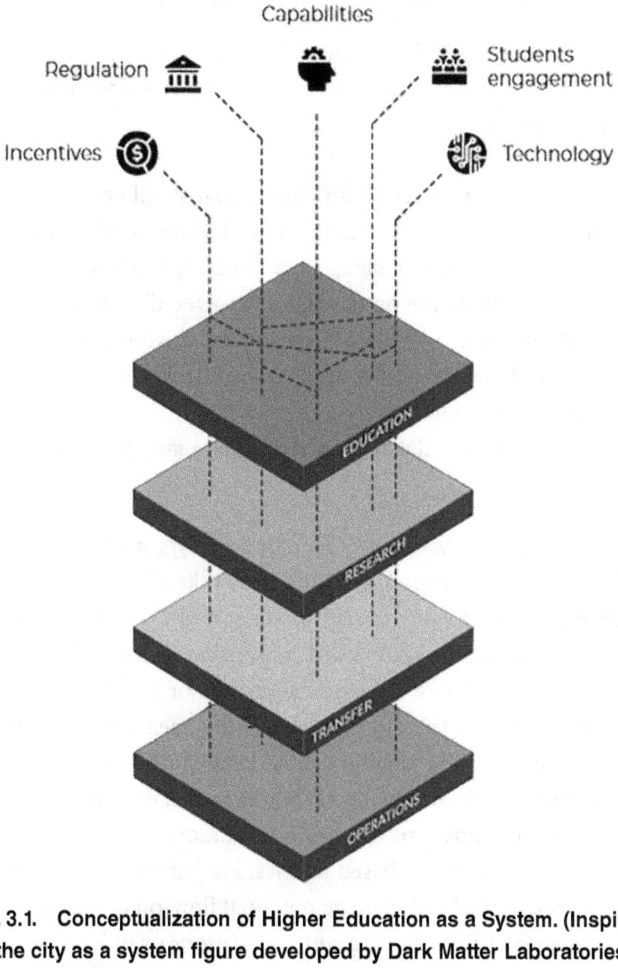

Fig. 3.1. Conceptualization of Higher Education as a System. (Inspired by the city as a system figure developed by Dark Matter Laboratories for the EU's NetZeroCities Program.)

Fig. 3.1 shows, as a general example without embracing the specificity of diverse contexts, the following four areas related to the HE mission:

- *Education*: formal and informal education, subjects, programs, life-long learning, executive education, etc.
- *Research*: fundamental research, applied research, innovation, etc.
- *Transfer*: transdisciplinary work with different stakeholders (private companies, governments, other research centres, civil society).
- *Operations*: electricity consumption/production, heating and cooling systems, food consumption, mobility, cultural and leisure activities, etc.

It also shows the main levers for change that should be used simultaneously for any systemic change. They include regulation, incentives, technology, student engagement, and capabilities.

Scaling up HE action on the SDGs involves all parts of this system, and mapping out the system and its drivers can provide a more nuanced understanding of the causes of the barriers to action and how to overcome them.

Some examples of the benefits this system mapping can provide include:

- *Identifying and managing conflicts, tradeoffs, and spillovers*: Because of the interconnected nature of the HE systems, attempts to address a barrier in one part of the system may lead to negative or unintended consequences in another part of the system, and may therefore be resisted or lead to negative spillover effects. Therefore, implementing measures to overcome barriers to SDG action should explicitly account for and address flow-on consequences. For example, in order to change academic incentives to rely less on traditional metrics and more on SDG impact-based metrics, institutions would also need to consider and manage potential flow-on consequences to the success in research grant applications or university rankings that are based on traditional metrics, or to the career implications for academics who have little experience or opportunity to engage in impact-based research.

- *Identifying levers for system-wide change*: Conversely, a systems view can help us identify levers of change that could help overcome barriers across the system. Common examples of levers include regulation, incentives (accreditation systems, recruitment processes, salary benefits, etc.), technology (classroom tech, learning management systems, data, etc.), governance (decision-making process, board of trustees, advisory boards, and partnerships with external stakeholders), student engagement (during the education process, as teaching assistants, as alumni), and capabilities (leadership training, professional development for staff and Faculty, etc.)
- *Avoiding actions that perpetuate an unsustainable system*: Improving parts of the system without a previous analysis of how the system itself works and whether it is unsustainable by design, may result in fragmented efficiency upgrades that perpetuate the unsustainable system itself. Without a clear long-term objective these small and fragmented changes risk locking institutions into an overall unsustainable model. Moving to a different system later may end up requiring more drastic changes that could also be more costly both financially as well as politically. For example, attempting to incentivize research for the SDGs by adding an SDG keyword dimension to traditional publication metrics (e.g. Elsevier & RELX, 2020) might provide valuable information on the topics being researched. However, this can also contribute to perpetuating a deeper issue, which is that over-reliance on measuring academic success through academic publications is itself a significant barrier to the kind of research that is needed for real-world impact on the SDGs (e.g. Care et al., 2021).

4.2. Defining the Outcomes

A central feature of the system change approaches discussed at the start of this section is to first identify specific and measurable desired outcomes, or what 'good' looks like, and then work backwards to define pathways to achieve these outcomes. The current definitions of what 'good' looks like in terms of HE contributions to the SDGs are inadequate, and this is hampering greater HE engagement with the SDGs. While this is a very complex issue, we believe it is important for HEIs – and the sector more broadly – to tackle this question explicitly.

Having specific and measurable targets to guide system transformation for the SDGs in HE is important because they underpin every part of the process, including:

- Clarifying what needs to change in practice in the HE system and by how much.
- Bringing all stakeholders on board to a shared vision.
- Identifying the pathways for getting there, including whether there are different pathways for reaching the same outcomes.
- Setting priorities for action.
- Measuring progress – to understand whether we are on track and when we have 'gotten there'.
- Motivating key stakeholders to take action – vague calls for action, even if supported, might be interpreted in a minimal way.
- Developing the key knowledge and tools that are needed to overcome some of the specific barriers to action, such as what SDG-related knowledge and skills every student should graduate with, or how to measure SDG impact (a 'keystone' barrier affecting incentives, funding criteria, institutional KPIs, etc.).

The SDGs and the Paris Agreement can provide overarching targets for what HE (and other sectors) should be aiming to achieve, but these can be tricky to apply in a HE context. While there have been many attempts (including our own) to define what good HE contributions to the SDGs should look like (e.g. Cuesta-Claros et al., 2022; Elsevier, 2022; Giesenbauer & Müller-Christ, 2020; SDSN, 2020; SDSN Australia/Pacific, 2017; UNESCO, 2022), our observation is that these are often vague (e.g. conceptual rather than specific), misplaced (e.g. focusing on HE activities or outputs, rather than on the outcomes and contributions to the SDGs), or contested (e.g. offering targets or a vision for HE contributions to the SDGs that is not universally accepted).

To some extent, this is inevitable: HE fulfils many different (and sometimes competing) roles, of which contributions to the SDGs are just one part; there are diverse visions of the type of role HE should take on in addressing the SDGs or to what extent (Cuesta-Claros et al., 2022); the global SDG targets are not designed to account for the indirect and varied contributions of HE; and each institution is likely to focus on a different set of actions, depending on its context and strengths.

While setting goals and targets to guide the transformation of HE globally may be difficult, goal setting is a crucial way to guide transformations. Without this, we risk that initiatives will continue to be insufficiently ambitious or that less than adequate solutions take hold (e.g. Bautista-Puig et al., 2022). We therefore propose that HEIs work individually and collectively on defining ambitious long-term vision and targets. Ideally, this can lead to a process of knowledge sharing across different institutions and ultimately a definition of a more robust, global vision on how to respond to the SDGs.

4.3. Employing Adaptive Leadership Approaches

Building on the seminal work of Heifetz et al. (2009), we suggest that most of the problems and barriers to HE action on the SDGs described in this chapter constitute adaptive challenges, which need adaptive leadership.

Heifetz et al. (2009) highlight the need to distinguish between technical and adaptive challenges in order to identify the most appropriate approach to solutions and implementation (Table 3.1).

Technical problems are those where both the definition of the problem and the solutions needed are clear (can be implemented by current know-how), and the primary responsibility for the work relies on a formal authority. For instance, if you break your leg, you need to go to the doctor, who can fix it through a complex but well-established surgery that will solve the challenge. The definition of

Table 3.1. Differences Between Technical and Adaptive Problems.

Kind of Work	Problem Definition	Solutions and Implementation	Primary Focus of Responsibility for the Work
Technical	Clear	Clear	Authority
Technical and adaptive	Clear	Requires learning	Authority and stakeholders
Adaptive	Requires learning	Requires learning	Stakeholders → Authority

Source: Adapted from Heifetz et al. (2009).

the problem and solutions are clear, and the physician has all the knowledge and technical tools to solve it.

Adaptive problems are those where the definition of the problem is unclear and needs constant learning; solutions are complex, varied, change over time, and require learning; and the work to address the challenge needs both formal authority and other stakeholders involved. For instance, if you suffer a heart attack, you should go to the doctor, who could do a complex surgery to fix the physical problems. However, you may also need to change your habits and way of life, and the solution needs to be learnt with the participation of many different stakeholders (you as patient, your family, your friends, etc.). The implications of this, as explained by Heifetz et al. (2009, p.24), are that:

> *Adaptive challenges can only be addressed through changes in people's priorities, beliefs, habits, and loyalties. Making progress requires going beyond any authoritative expertise to mobilize discovery, shedding certain entrenched ways, tolerating losses, and generating the new capacity to thrive anew.*

Adaptive leadership is 'the practice of mobilizing people to tackle tough challenges and thrive' (Heifetz et al., 2009, p. 21), and consists of:

- Continuous learning about the context, process, and problems you are facing.
- Mapping out the different stakeholders relevant to the problem, including a profound assessment of the values, interests,

loyalties, gains, and loses that are associated to them in relation to transforming the system.

- Orchestrating multiple stakeholder priorities to define thriving, and then realizing it.
- Creating safe spaces where diverse stakeholders can have difficult conversations and co-create solutions to challenges using collective intelligence.
- Adopting an experimental mindset.
- Identifying the few needs for change, and predicting the reaction from the system, stakeholders, and individuals.

In summary, adaptive leadership is an iterative process involving (1) observation of stakeholders, events, and patterns around the problem; (2) interpretation of all the elements in the system; (3) design of interventions based on the observations and interpretations; and (4) implement those interventions by evaluating them as they are implemented and re-formulating them according with new observations and interpretations.

Adaptive leadership could be an effective method for university leaders to analyze and address the adaptive problems described in Section 3. However, adaptive leadership is not easy, partly because it may be counter intuitive if analyzed through the lenses of traditional leadership theory, and because it requires some mind changing and developing capabilities to follow the above-mentioned process.

4.4. Investing in Building Genuine Partnerships

A key aspect of adaptive leadership (Section 4.3) is that it seeks the engagement and support of other stakeholders. There is overwhelming agreement that adaptive problems cannot be addressed effectively by one individual, organization, or even country. The complexity and scale of adaptive problems require working in partnership. Furthermore, as we have been arguing in this chapter, these problems are most effectively understood, diagnosed, and addressed through the optics of systems analysis. Systems are, by definition, composed of multiple individuals, processes, and organizations that interact with each other. Therefore, the impact that one piece of the system can have on an adaptive problem is limited. In this section, we focus on the importance of meaningful partnerships that will be at the centre of any deep transformation of HE.

Fig. 3.2, developed by the University of Pretoria (2019), graphically shows how to think about the most effective type of partnerships to address a problem. The University of Pretoria proposes two variables that can help determine what type of partnership to establish: the nature of the problems we face (technical or adaptive; discrete or multifaceted; and simple or complex), and the type of solution this problem may require, including the type(s) of knowledge needed to address it.

Adaptive problems, which are complex, multifaceted challenges that require different types of knowledge and the involvement of different stakeholders, will require more transformative, or 'genuine', partnerships. The example presented in Section 4.3 of how a medical procedure requires not just medical knowledge but also changes in behaviour, the involvement of a support system, etc., shows the importance of such partnerships in achieving success.

To be effective, these genuine partnerships may require a long period of 'getting to know each other', to reach an understanding of shared values and purpose that can guide the design of a joint body of work. The process of establishing functional genuine partnerships can take much longer than transactional partnerships, the latter being typically determined by a written contract, with clear timelines, deliverables and boundaries determining how risk and outcomes will be shared. However, genuine or transformational partnerships can, in turn, be quicker to adapt to changing contexts and be more opportunistic and innovative. In that sense, they can also be more resilient and potentially have large-scale impact.

According to Austin (2000), these two types of partnerships intertwine with each other. We shouldn't think about them as a complete dichotomy but, rather, along a spectrum of collaboration. In that sense, the arrows pointing across quadrants in Fig. 3.2 could be interpreted as a gradient where transactional and

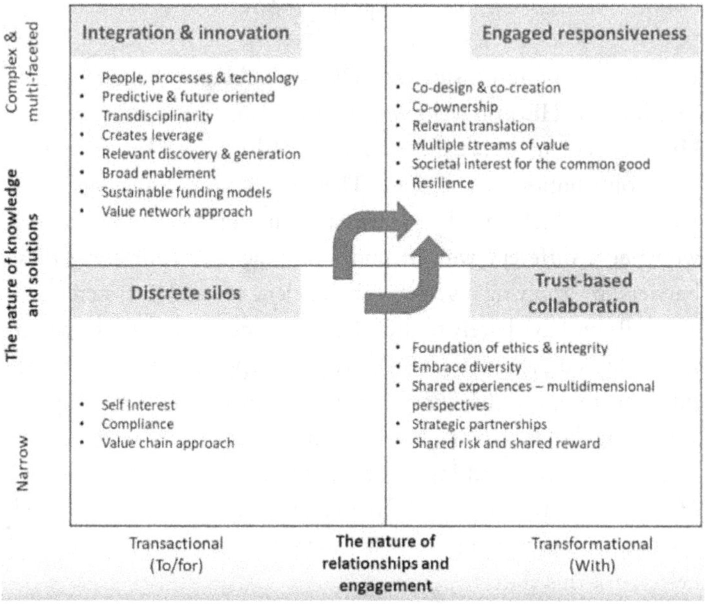

Fig. 3.2. The University of Pretoria Approach to Creating Transformational Change.

Reproduced with permission from University of Pretoria (2019).

transformational partnerships co-exist. Typically, the nature of the relationship between partners evolves as the partners get to know each other, develop effective working mechanisms and as they decide to face more complex problems that require more flexibility.

It is possible that a specific institution starts by exploring adaptive problems through relationships that, while still in the transactional phase, explore a certain level of integration across organizations, which shows the value of a network model of engagement. As these experiences work, partners may decide to experiment further, such as by perhaps moving to a less transactional approach for one key project.

These types of genuine partnerships, which bridge across disciplines and sectors by bringing these actors to jointly define their scope of work and objectives, can help promote systemic solutions based on consensus. Including diverse groups can provide a more sophisticated and granular vision of the problem and guarantee that solutions leave no one behind.

5. CONCLUSIONS

The urgency of addressing the SDGs and climate change, and the centrality of HE in developing the solutions, mean that we need HEIs to become much more focused and engaged on scaling up their contributions to the SDGs. There are many specific barriers to doing this, which have been seemingly intractable. In this chapter, we offer a different way of understanding and addressing these barriers, by applying a systems change lens to the HE system.

While we have barely scratched the surface in terms of the potential of this lens, and many of the proposed approaches require careful effort to apply, this chapter begins a conversation that requires many stakeholders to effectively continue. Our purpose and call to action here is the need for the sector to start viewing the challenge of engaging HE on the SDGs in a much more ambitious, nuanced, systematic, and systemic way. We hope the ideas we presented will help spark this shift.

REFERENCES

Austin, J. E. (2000). Strategic collaboration between nonprofits and business. *Nonprofit and Voluntary Sector Quarterly*, *29*(1), 69–97. http://doi.org/10.1177/0899764000773746346

Bautista-Puig, N., Orduña-Malea, E., & Perez-Esparrells, C. (2022). Enhancing sustainable development goals or promoting universities? An analysis of the Times Higher Education Impact Rankings. *International Journal of Sustainability in Higher Education*, *23*(8), 211–231. http://doi.org/10.1108/IJSHE-07-2021-0309

Browett, H., & Denis-Ryan, A. (2021, December 13). *Applying system change methodology to drive ambitious climate action.* Climateworks Centre. https://www.climateworkscentre.org/news/applying-system-change-methodology-to-drive-ambitious-climate-action/

Care, O., Bernstein, M. J., Chapman, M., Diaz Reviriego, I., Dressler, G., Felipe-Lucia, M. R., Friis, C., Graham, S., Hänke, H., Haider, L. J., Hernández-Morcillo, M. Hoffmann, H., Kernecker, M., Nicol, P. Piñeiro, C. Pitt, H., Schill, C., Seufert, V., Shu, K., Valencia, V., & Zaehringer, J. G.

(2021). Creating leadership collectives for sustainability transformations. *Sustainability Science*, 16, 703–708. https://doi.org/10.1007/s11625-021-00909-y

Cuesta-Claros, A., Malekpour, S., Raven, R., & Kestin, T. (2022). Understanding the roles of universities for sustainable development transformations: A framing analysis of university models. *Sustainable Development*, *30*(4), 525–538. https://doi.org/10.1002/sd.2247

Ellis, R., Patton, I., Gill, J., & Ross, J. (2022, May 3). *Impact rankings 2022: Results announced*. Times Higher Education. https://www.timeshighereducation.com/news/impact-rankings-2022-results-announced

Elsevier. (2022). *The impact rankings, Scopus and SciVal: A closer look for university leaders*. Retrieved October 18, 2022, from https://www.elsevier.com/research-intelligence/impact-rankings-data

Elsevier & RELX. (2020). *The power of data to advance the SDGs: Mapping research for the sustainable development goals*. Elsevier Research Analytics Group and the RELX SDG Resource Centre.

European Commission, Directorate-General for Research and Innovation. (2020). *100 Climate-neutral cities by 2030 – by and for the citizens: Interim report of the mission board for climate-neutral and smart cities*. Publications Office. https://data.europa.eu/doi/10.2777/62649

European Commission, Directorate-General for Research and Innovation. (2021). *EU* mission climate-neutral and smart cities implementation plan. https://research-and-innovation.ec.europa.eu/document/download/d2eb2069-3b4a-4015-9801-7daab749d31b_en?filename=cities_mission_implementation_plan.pdf

FABLE. (2020). Pathways to sustainable land-use and food systems. 2020 Report of the FABLE Consortium. International Institute for Applied Systems Analysis (IIASA) and Sustainable Development Solutions Network (SDSN). https://doi.org/10.22022/ESM/12-2020.16896

Giesenbauer, B., & Müller-Christ, G. (2020). University 4.0: Promoting the transformation of higher education institutions toward sustainable development. *Sustainability*, *12*(8), 3371. https://doi.org/10.3390/su12083371

Grin, J., Rotmans, J., & Schot, J. (2010). *Transitions to sustainable development: New directions in the study of long term transformative change*. Routledge.

Heifetz, R. A., Grashow, A., & Linsky, M. (2009). *The practice of adaptive leadership: Tools and tactics for changing your organization and the world*. Harvard Business Press.

Horan, D. (2019). A new approach to partnerships for SDG transformations. *Sustainability*, *11*, 4947. https://doi.org/10.3390/su11184947

Kotter, J. (2012). Accelerate! *Harvard Business Review*, *90*(11), 44–58.

Leal Filho, W., Wu, Y. C. J., Brandli, L. L., Avila, L. V., Azeiteiro, U. M., Caeiro, S., & da Rosa Gama Madruga, L. R. (2017). Identifying and overcoming obstacles to the implementation of sustainable development at universities. *Journal of Integrative Environmental Sciences*, *14*, 93–108. https://doi.org/10.1080/1943815X.2017.1362007

OECD & SDSN. (2019). *Long-term pathways for the implementation of the SDGs: The governance implications* (Reflection Paper July 2019). OECD & SDSN.

Purcell, W. M., & Haddock-Fraser, J. (2023). *Handbook of sustainability in higher education: An agenda for transformational change*. Bloomsbury Press.

Sachs, J. D., Lafortune, G., Kroll, C., Fuller, G., & Woelm, F. (2022). *Sustainable development report 2022: From crisis to sustainable development: The SDGs as a roadmap to 2030 and beyond*. Cambridge University Press. http://doi.org/10.1017/9781009210058

Sachs, J. D., Schmidt-Traub, G., Mazzucato, M., Messner, D., Nakicenovic, N., & Rockström, J. (2019). Six transformations to achieve the sustainable development goals. *Nature Sustainability*, *2*(9), 805–814.

Sachs, J. D., & Thwaites, J. (2022, September 1). *Reflecting on 10 years of SDSN*. Sustainable Development Solutions Network. https://www.unsdsn.org/reflecting-on-10-years-of-sdsn

Sustainable Development Solutions Network (SDSN). (2020). *Accelerating education for the SDGs in universities: A guide for universities, colleges, and tertiary and higher education institutions*. SDSN.

SDSN Australia/Pacific. (2017). *Getting started with the SDGs in universities: A guide for universities, higher education institutions, and the academic sector* (Australia, New Zealand and Pacific ed.). Sustainable Development Solutions Network – Australia/Pacific.

SDSN Secretariat. (2022, April 27). *University sector support to the UN's decade of action – A meeting of university presidents in the Americas.* Sustainable Development Solutions Network. https://www.unsdsn.org/a-meeting-of-university-presidents-in-the-americas

TWI2050 – The World in 2050. (2018). Transformations to achieve the sustainable development goals. Report prepared by the World in 2050 initiative. International Institute for Applied Systems Analysis (IIASA). www.twi2050.org

United Nations. (2022). *The sustainable development goals report 2022.* United Nations. https://unstats.un.org/sdgs/report/2022/

UNESCO. (2022). *Knowledge-driven actions: transforming higher education for global sustainability.* UNESCO Global Independent Expert Group on the Universities and the 2030 Agenda, UNESCO. https://unesdoc.unesco.org/ark:/48223/pf0000380519

University of Pretoria. (2019). *Sustainable development report 2019.* University of Pretoria.

4

TOWARDS GLOBAL EQUITY IN HIGHER EDUCATION

Joanna Newman

ABSTRACT

Without the contribution of the higher education (HE) sector, none of the United Nations (UN) Sustainable Development Goals (SDG) are achievable. Through research, teaching, and community engagement, universities globally make vital contributions towards Agenda 30. Through partnerships, their impact is enhanced – university networks are key to facilitating collaboration. The Association of Commonwealth Universities (ACU) is a global university network encompassing more than 500 universities. ACU spans five continents with membership representative of the full diversity of the Commonwealth. University networks such as this demonstrate that bringing institutions together enhances their ability to tackle global challenges. University networks are vital vehicles for knowledge sharing and best practice. ACU members in low- to middle-income countries face systematic biases that need significant support for disparities to decrease. The ACU provides a platform for all its members, including in the global South, to have their voices heard and affect policy-makers at the most prominent forums, including the Commonwealth Heads of Government

Meeting (CHOGM), the Conference of Commonwealth Education Ministers (CCEM), and the Conference of the Parties (COP). The ACU implements initiatives that build capacity. Examples include Climate Impacts Research Capacity and Leadership Enhancement (CIRCLE), which supports researchers and institutions across Africa to produce internationally peer reviewed research into the climate change; and Partnership for Enhanced and Blended Learning (PEBL), which works with universities in Africa to enhance access to quality education through blended learning. These projects rank alongside similar initiatives that leverage networks to deliver outcomes that would not otherwise be possible. Without networks such as these, the great potential of universities to tackle the SDGs will likely not be realised.

Keywords: Commonwealth; collaboration; networks; development; knowledge exchange; mobility

In 2015 the SDGs gave the world a 'shared blueprint for peace and prosperity for people and the planet' (United Nations, n.d.b) – a blueprint that, for the first time, included tertiary education. This was a significant move: HE was notably missing from the SDGs' predecessors – the Millennium Development Goals (MDGs) – both as a development goal in itself and as driver to address development challenges more broadly (The Association of Commonwealth Universities, 2015).

Reflecting on the MDGs – both the progress made and gaps which remained – the then Secretary-General of the United Nations Ban Ki-moon wrote: 'Achieving the SDGs will require an even stronger global partnership, complemented by multistakeholder partnerships to mobilize and share knowledge, expertise, technology, and financial resources' (United Nations, 2015). This chapter aims to demonstrate the key role of university networks like the ACU in facilitating precisely these sorts of vital partnerships and knowledge exchange.

The explicit acknowledgement of HE, and crucially the right to access it, as a global development goal in itself is outlined under SDG4: quality education, and the targets which underpin it (United Nations, 2015). These include equal access for all to affordable and quality tertiary education, including university (4.3), education that delivers the necessary skills for employment and entrepreneurship (4.4), the elimination of gender and other disparities in accessing education at all levels (4.5), and the expansion of the number of scholarships for university study (4B). These targets are both welcome and ambitious.

And yet the SDGs are deeply interconnected and should not be viewed in Isolation – indeed, the UN itself reminds us that 'a lack of progress on one goal hinders progress on others' (UN Global Compact, n.d.). HE in particular underpins all 17 SDGs – goals that will require skilled scientists, doctors, lawmakers, researchers, and teachers at every level to achieve them. This, in turn, circles back to SDG4 and its targets: such a workforce can only be provided by universities and, in particular, universities that are able to reach and teach the most innovative, capable, and hardworking individuals their countries can produce – individuals who may, without support, be unable to access the education that would make full use of their potential. The potential contribution of such individuals is something the world cannot afford to waste.

While the inclusion of tertiary education marked a sea change in the global development agenda, this recognition of HE's contribution to sustainable development more broadly cannot be taken for granted. International summits on global development – as well as international bodies such as the Tony Blair Institute for Global Change (Time for a World Education Service: Focused, Free and for All, n.d.) – frequently foreground the importance of education, but it is often the case that primary and secondary schooling take centre stage, with HE treated as competition against the need for universal basic literacy. Such a goal is, of course, essential, but to leave tertiary education off the priority list is a serious and short-sighted mistake: early and HE are not an either/or, but necessary complements to each other in an intellectual ecosystem where the prosperity and stability of nations frequently depends on their possession of a strong body of skilled and educated citizens.

This status quo may be starting to shift, however. At the 21st CCEM in Nairobi in 2022, Ministers stated: 'We acknowledge that tertiary education is vital to sustainable development and that universities play a critical role within the Commonwealth education ecosystem, and that they can contribute positively towards all aspects of economic and social development and the successful realization of all 17 UN SDGs'. The ministerial statement endorsed the recommendations submitted to ministers by the ACU (The Association of Commonwealth Universities, n.d.a), calling for increased investment in quality tertiary education. These recommendations were later submitted to the CHOGM, sounding a clarion call on a global stage.

From developing vaccines against global pandemics to drought-resistant crops that can withstand an environmentally uncertain future, universities are at the centre of scientific breakthroughs. As more and more jobs become dependent on education, they create generations of potential employees with the qualifications and skills to take on profitable work, benefitting not only themselves but also their families and communities, as well as their nations' economies as a whole. Indeed, while the length of this chapter doesn't allow for exploration of the link between Gross Tertiary Enrolment (GTE) and gross domestic product, a more robust understanding of the correlation between the two is surely an area worthy of investigation, given the implications for investment in HE.

Furthermore, universities are centrepoints of social understanding, engaging with communities and bringing their knowledge to bear on issues of inequality and inclusion, as well as teaching their graduates the kind of critical thinking that challenges the limits of in-group polarization and encourages a more open, cooperative, and big picture view of the world (Newman, 2022a).

In addition, universities are one of the best opportunities for young people to expose themselves to other cultures through international mobility – the opportunity to study or work in another country. Studying abroad, being daily exposed to the realities of another nation, can be a revelation for the individual, but on a wider scale, it also creates a societal value (Newman, 2022). With an increasingly global job market, students able to take on work in internationally collaborative settings bring benefits to both their own communities and those they interact with. A large body of culturally agile, well-informed, and internationally connected workers is the global asset needed to address global crises. These are, after all, citizens of the international community, and the more aware an individual is about the lives and cultures of others, the more they have to contribute to the world.

The reality is, however, that more needs to be done. Universities are far from immune to international inequalities, and as long as access to quality education is uneven, those inequalities are maintained. The Covid-19 pandemic has only heightened the urgency (A National Education Opportunities Network (UK) World Access to Higher Education Day, 2021): the health crisis led to an education crisis as safely attending classes became ever more difficult, to the detriment of both the physical and psychological well-being of students.

In May 2020, the ACU ran a survey of digital engagement across 33 countries, with 258 respondents in all (The Association of Commonwealth Universities, 2020a). The findings indicated severe disruption caused by the Covid-19 pandemic: 52% of respondents reported that their campus had been closed entirely, and 45% reported partial closure, while 78% said that the pandemic had a negative impact on their ability to undertake research. Digital learning was the clear centrepoint of efforts to counter this: 80% reported that some, or most, of the university's teaching had been moved online, and 69% reported that they had been able to take their research activities online as well.

Internet access, in short, was vital to a substantial majority of respondents' abilities to carry on in the face of crisis – and as there is no guarantee that Covid-19 will be the last pandemic the world faces, a solid foundation of online learning remains crucial to universities' disaster preparedness. However, there is a marked digital divide between nations: while 83% of respondents from high income countries reported having broadband access, the figure dropped to 63% for upper middle countries, 38% for lower middle-income countries, and a dismaying 19% for low-income countries. It was these poorer nations that were unable to move to online learning. Researchers, meanwhile, showed a divide based on internet access: among those with a broadband connection, 33% strongly agreed that the pandemic had hampered their ability to research, but for those without, the figure jumped to 43%. The practical fact is that Covid-19 hit far harder for university teachers and students who were not in a position to use the Internet to fill in the gaps left by campus closures.

More than that, the survey revealed a 'double digital divide' in tertiary education: the lower the standing of an individual, the less likely they were to have access to much-needed broadband. A total of 74% of senior leaders had such access, followed by 52% of professional services, and both groups reported that they were provided institutional contributions for devices or data at a rate of 82%. However, only 38% of academics, and 30% of students, reported having broadband, and were provided institutional contributions at a rate of 45% and 40%, respectively. Likewise, when reporting problems with remote working, senior leaders were less likely to report data costs (48%) and slow internet speeds (63%) than academics (68% and 74%, respectively). With affordability being an issue, especially in poorer countries, the younger and lower-ranked members of the university community were disproportionately affected.

Particularly unfortunate from the point of view of achieving the SDGs, the natural, environmental, and earth sciences have been particularly set back: 92% of academics in these disciplines reported that the pandemic affected their ability to research, as compared with only 61% in the arts, social sciences, and humanities. It is urgent that these subjects are made more pandemic proof in the future, as sustainability depends upon them.

Even after the pandemic, its effects on learning will linger: only 25% of respondents said they worked online weekly prior to the pandemic, and 16% said that they never had, but after the pandemic, the number who anticipate never working online dropped to 1%. A total of 65% of respondents anticipated working online frequently in the future. The will to develop high-quality online learning is there throughout the academic world – this was agreed by 89% of respondents – but the situation is in urgent need of improvement. By now, millions are at risk of dropping out of university – and, since the most vulnerable and marginalized are most at risk, for many this will mean dropping back into poverty. Education is a key part of human development and needs an integrated approach.

In addition, it is clear more needs to be done to ensure that universities from low- and middle-income nations are enabled to develop and grow. 'Small states' – of which there are 32 in the Commonwealth (The Association on Commonwealth Universities, 2021) – are particularly vulnerable to development challenges and climate change; they are also often the places whose expertise can most contribute the knowledge the international community needs to hear.

However, there currently exists a systemic bias towards universities from wealthier nations. A study published in 2020 (Skopec et al., 2020) reviewed 3,501 titles and found that abstracts from higher income countries were rated as more relevant to their research subject, and more likely to be recommended to colleagues, than abstracts from lower income countries. Papers from nations on the sharp edge of environmental crisis, in short, were less likely to be taken seriously – a disastrous implication for everyone. Papers on the subject of computer science were also significantly more likely to be accepted for presentation at a conference if they came under the imprimatur of a 'Top University' – a concept inextricably entangled with colonial history. As a paper presented at the second International RESUP Conference in 2009 put it, 'the organisation of higher education and research systems is always the heritage of a national history', observing that the inequalities faced by universities include financial and symbolic resources, the students, academics, and partners they can attract, the degree of autonomy from public authorities, and the stability and prosperity of the region in which they operate.

In addition, universities do not act in isolation from the job market: as Theocharis Kromydas (2017) observed that education has expanded rapidly since World War II, there is a constant tension between education as a means of developing human capacity for its own sake and education as a method of producing appropriate workers for a capitalist economy. A 'constant marketization of education', Kromydas points out, makes degrees less affordable for poorer students, including those from low-income regions, while leaving them also at greater risk of poverty in a job market where well-paid work for those without degrees is increasingly hard to come by – adding up to students from less wealthy backgrounds being 'vastly disadvantaged'.

It is also important for universities to recognize that, even in the most technologically advanced and prosperous nations, students of colour and indigenous students face particular challenges when it comes to participation in university life. In an episode of *The Internationalist*, a podcast produced by the ACU (The Association of Commonwealth Universities, n.d.), the President of the UK's National Union of Students Larissa Kennedy described universities as 'spaces that were never built by, nor for, us', positing that independent spaces that 'center Black healing' were ultimately likely to achieve more. While Candace Brunette-Debassige, Acting Vice-Provost and Associate Vice-President of Indigenous Initiatives at Western University, Canada, presented a more hopeful view of universities, she agreed that 'decolonising … or indigenising from within' was a continual struggle. Both agreed that universities could be a hostile space to marginalized students, with racism, microaggressions, and a lack of role models in positions of authority creating considerable stress. At a more systemic level, both also agreed that while a black or indigenous lecturer could act as a 'beacon', the inherent structure of universities, with single teacher figures acting as arbiters of knowledge and students set in competition with one another, was a culture alien to the very goals of decolonization.

Unfortunately, our colleagues in lower income countries also report that the old system of 'research dissemination' – that is to say, sharing findings in scholarly journals and assuming they will reach the appropriate ears – is stacked against them (Newman, 2022). Chang Da Wang of the National Higher Education Research Unite at the Universiti Sains Malaysia, for example, comments that 'universities are … brought to their knees by global university rankings' (Chang Da Wan, 2021), dependent on publication in international journals that universities must pay 'thousands in subscription fees to access'. Da Wang observes that, as the focus in lower income nations is also often to produce graduates employable by the standards of former colonial powers, the final effect can be less like equal inclusion in a collaborative venture than a form of recolonization.

Even in wealthy nations, however, most academics find the current system of research policy is difficult because it only rewards high numbers of publications in high-impact journals – which is impossible to achieve without university resources, but also means that the kind of applied research, involving different funding sources and partners, and which is most useful to charities and climate action bodies, is less favoured.

These are voices the ACU takes very seriously, as they are crucial for global progress. We strongly discourage a defensive response from Western readers: a diversity of viewpoints does not attack the pre-existing curriculum, but instead enriches it in the best academic tradition, broadening its understanding to include the many new different types of knowledge that are worth preserving and spreading.

An example of the value of such knowledge sharing can be found in the Commonwealth Blue Charter. In 2018 (Commonwealth, n.d.), all 56 Commonwealth countries agreed upon this commitment to sustainable oceans; one third of the world's coastal oceans 45% of the world's coral reefs are in the Commonwealth, and to tackle the rising temperature and acidity of the seas, the need for a concerted effort was recognized. To advance an ambitious programme for protecting the vital marine ecosystem, 10 action groups were founded (Commonwealth, n.d.): the Commonwealth Clean Ocean Alliance, led by the UK and Vanatu, which tackles plastic pollution; Coral Reef Protection and Restoration, led by Australia, Belize, and Mauritius; Mangrove Ecosystems and Livelihood, led by Sri Lanka; Marine Protected Areas, led by Barbados and Seychelles; Ocean Acidification, led by New Zealand; Ocean and Climate Change, led by Fiji; Ocean Observation, led by Canada; Sustainable Aquaculture, led by Cyprus; Sustainable Blue Economy, led by Antigua, Barbuda, and Kenya; and Sustainable Costal Fisheries, led by Maldives and Kiribati.

The ACU supported this initiative (which links directly to SDG14: Life Below Water), by securing funding from the UK Department for Business, Energy, and Industrial Strategy and Waitrose & Partners for the ACU Blue Charter Fellowships Programme, between 2018 and 2021 supported 48 outstanding researchers to work in the fields of keeping the seas plastic-free, developing plastic alternatives, and cleaning up the plastic already polluting the oceans at a rate of 8 million tonnes per year (The Association of Commonwealth Universities, n.d.). These grants have been issued across continents, including researchers

(The Association of Commonwealth Universities, n.d.) from India, Malawi, Nigeria, South Africa, Canada, and Australia, bringing in a wide range of talent.

The Living Lands Charter, for another example, set out a major commitment in June 2022 to preserve the biodiversity of planet Earth and noted that local and Indigenous communities frequently employ practices and traditions that show a more far-sighted and sustainable approach to the natural world, as well as providing essential on-the-ground guardianship of vulnerable ecosystems (The Commonwealth, 2022). Many Indigenous communities already model responsible stewardship of the land – but if research cannot bring their knowledge to policy-makers, then the positive change they might represent will not happen.

An international community where lower income nations are struck harder by crises, yet struggle to make their expertise heard, fails everyone. In order to achieve the goals of Agenda 30, universities need to work in full partnership. A sound and well-set-out strategy of collaboration is crucial for the future. A study published in January 2022 (The Association of Commonwealth Universities, 2022a) by the ACU and the British Council found that HE partnerships make a significant contribution to achieving all 17 of these goals – and that in particular, interdisciplinary approaches are critical, given that the SDGs are interlinked. We find that three factors are key when it comes to delivering on the SDGs (Joanna Newman, 2022): universities in every nation need adequate funding and resources; opportunities to access tertiary education must be made available to everyone who would benefit; and, finally, no one SDG can be achieved in isolation. By bringing together multiple disciplines, sectors, and countries on an equal footing, international partnerships are our best chance.

Founded in 1913, the ACU is the world's first international university network and the only accredited Commonwealth body representing HE. Its stated mission is to build a better world through HE, with a global community that today encompasses around 500 universities, over 10 million students and a million staff members over 50 countries. The ACU spans five continents; 76% of our member universities are in low- and middle-income countries. Over the past 60 years, it has produced over 90,000 alumni; it awards around £650,000 in grants and scholarships annually, and at any one time, there are 3,500 students studying on ACU-administered scholarships (The Association of Commonwealth Universities, 2021).

Since its founding, the ACU has continually moved with the times, making maximum use of the pre-existing ties of Commonwealth nations while moving past its colonial origins to a more egalitarian collaboration between nations. Originally founded as the Universities Bureau of the British Empire (The Association of Commonwealth Universities, n.d.), with 53 universities enrolled, it was renamed the Association of Universities of the British Commonwealth in 1948 – the same year the Commonwealth Charter identified its core principles as 'consensus and common action, mutual respect, inclusiveness, transparency, accountability, legitimacy, and responsiveness' with an explicit commitment to act as a 'champion of small states' (Commonwealth Charter, n.d.).

These are aspirational goals rather than a description of what has already been achieved, but they remain the foundation of the modern Commonwealth, which seeks to recognize its history of empire but now work together as a modern organization. These are the values the ACU seeks to uphold. Granted a Royal Charter under the new name of the ACU in 1963 (its jubilee year) (The Association of Commonwealth Universities, n.d.), the ACU now faces the future as a modern and collaborative institution.

Access to HE has increased greatly since the World War II and is now a crucial requirement in most work environments, but regional disparities in tertiary enrolment around the world mirror global inequalities. By 2030, Australia, Canada, and the UK are expected to reach a GTE of 90%, while Japan and Korea expect to have a university enrolment rate of 80% among their high school graduates by 2050. In sub-Saharan Africa, however, where 70% of the population is under the age of 30, the GTE lags at only 8%; and by 2050, nations such as the Central African Republic and Niger are expected to still be struggling to reach a rate of 5%. The 54 member states of the Commonwealth are home to a third of the world's young people, from the most prosperous countries to the least: the ACU supports education reform to bring students in lower income nations to tertiary education where their capabilities can benefit global progress (The Association of Commonwealth Universities, 2021).

To advance its goals, ACU leads numerous initiatives to support universities in all aspects of their functioning – from institutional and administrative development to funding individuals and projects which contribute to the aims of the SDGs.

In particular – and with direct relevance to SDG target 4b – the ACU has an extensive history of promoting international student mobility – the chance to work or study in another country. We manage the UK government's three major scholarship schemes (ACU, n.d.), including the Commonwealth Scholarships (Commonwealth Scholarship Commission in the UK, n.d.) – which are explicitly led by international development objectives, as well as the Queen Elizabeth Commonwealth Scholarships (ACU, n.d.). The latter are unique in that they offer talented students from all parts of the Commonwealth the chance to undertake a Master's degree hosted at a university in a developing country, thereby creating new directions and new dynamics in international exchange.

Specific grants are offered to encourage diversity and inclusion, such as the gender and other disparities in education which SDG4.5 seeks to address. The ACU Gender Grants (ACU, n.d.), for instance, support university initiatives in areas such as tackling sexual harassment and violence on campus, supporting women in leadership roles and in science and research, creating effective institutional policies to ensure equal treatment, and making gender equity a cornerstone of the curriculum. The feedback has been tremendously positive; Hellen Adogo of the University of Johannesburg, South Africa, for example, reported that, 'the first cohort of female scholars unanimously agreed that the programme gave them the tools to plan their career development' (ACU, n.d.).

The ACU Summer School, meanwhile, brings Commonwealth students together to discuss global challenges through a dynamic programme of lectures, workshops, field trips, and group work – and is one of the many ways in which the ACU is addressing SDG4.7 ('By 2030, ensure that all learners acquire the knowledge and skills needed to promote sustainable development, including, among others, through education for sustainable development and sustainable lifestyles ... global citizenship and appreciation of cultural diversity'). The event takes place yearly at a different member university each time – with universities in Botswana, Cameroon, Canada, Ghana, Hong Kong, India, Malaysia, Mauritius, Rwanda, and the UK hosting the event to date. Bursaries are available to help a wide range of students to attend, with priority given to those who have not previously travelled beyond their own region. Students participating are exposed not only from talks by experts and academic and business leaders, but cultural events, day trips, and social activities: the purpose is not just to educate, but to give ambitious and enterprising young people – potential future leaders in their fields themselves – the chance to meet and make friends with others who come from widely different cultures.

These promising global citizens are able to connect with each other, work in union on shared group projects, and remain in touch after the Summer School ends, hopefully for the long term. At the most recent Summer School, held in 2022 in Leeds Trinity University in the UK, participants engaged in a friendly four-day contest to develop a sports-related initiative that could address the one of the SDGs in a specific community, as well as enjoying recreational time in each others' company. In the words of Masters' student JooYu Feng from Nanyang Technological University in Singapore: 'It was a great opportunity to meet new friends, learn about different cultures, and collaborate with people around the world on a project. I had a blast!' (ACU, 2022).

Another ACU initiative is the CIRCLE programme, which as well addressing goals such as SDG13 (Climate action) also directly addresses SDG4.7 – 'ensuring that all learners acquire the knowledge and skills needed to promote sustainable development' (United Nations, n.d.). Delivered with support from partners The African Academy of Sciences, Vitae, and the Natural Resources Institute at the University of Greenwich, CIRCLE is funded by the UK Foreign, Commonwealth and Development Office (ACU, n.d.), and employs innovative dual tactics: not only supporting individual academics in sub-Saharan Africa to undertake research in climate change across the continent, but also working with local universities so that their own capacity to support superior research is enhanced.

To promote the former, CIRCLE provides visiting fellowships: researchers early in their careers spend 12 months at another institution, giving them an opportunity to deepen and broaden their study of the subject. ACU ensures such Fellows are given a broad spectrum of support on three fronts: a Mentor from their home institution, a Supervisor from the institution they are visiting, and an Advisor from a third institution who acts as a specialist in their subject. Training and funding were also specifically ringfenced to help researchers get their work noticed by influential academic peers and political decision-makers, as well as local inhabitants of areas struggling with environmental damage.

A key component of every Fellow's project was to make sure that it ended with public engagement and exchange of ideas, getting the best chance to make a real impact beyond academia into policy and practical change. For instance, CIRCLE Fellow Doris Akachuḳwu has visited oil-producing regions of south-east Nigeria, meeting with communities in areas hit hard by soil pollution and providing practical advice on restoring the land to health. For another example, Mavis Akuffobea-Essilfie has managed outreach workshops in Ghana, bringing together local communities and policy-makers to further understanding of the specific impact climate change has upon women and girls (Newman, 2022).

These fellowships were multidisciplinary, ranging from water and energy to agricultural science and the socioeconomics of agriculture and rural livelihoods. Between 2015 and 2017, CIRCLE awarded 100 fellowships, 39 to Master's-qualified researchers and 61 to PhD-qualified researchers. Of these awards, exactly 50% were made to female academics.

Meanwhile, the Institutional Strengthening Programme (ISP), managed in partnership with Vitae, works to build stronger frameworks that will enable universities' core capacity to support research – research in general, and on climate change in particular. To date, 31 institutions across 10 countries have participated in the ISP, and an independent 2021 report described ACU's inputs as 'very high quality' (Kelly et al., 2021). CIRCLE continues to develop, and with a strong institutional foundation and public outreach as an integral part of the process, researchers who can bring their work forward to effect collaborative and sustainable change.

Another example of ACU's initiatives is PEBL, which directly supports the SDG4.3's commitment to increase access to quality and affordable tertiary education for all. Already successfully established in East Africa, including Uganda, Tanzania, Kenya, and Rwanda (ACU, n.d.), and with a two-year programme launched in West Africa in 2022, PEBL works to deliver education and training to more, and more diverse, students than would otherwise be possible (ACU, 2022).

PEBL's methods rely on blended learning – a combination of online and face-to-face teaching. This has had obvious benefits during the Covid-19 pandemic but is applicable far beyond. In many rural regions, for example, the distances students need to travel can be prohibitive, and universities can suffer from a shortage of lecturers (ACU, n.d.). By making remote learning possible for students and online modules available to bear some of the weight otherwise born by teaching staff, universities should be able to offer more education to more students in an affordable way; PEBL works with them to co-create programmes specifically suited to their needs. The West African PEBL programme will spread these benefits, planning by 2024 to have trained 100+ university staff as leaders to support their colleagues develop blended learning courses, 1,200 lecturers and 5,000 students, as well as teaching 3,000 students the soft skills to improve their employability (ACU, n.d.).

The challenges blended learning presents, however, are not to be underestimated (Newman, 2022). As PEBL participant Dr Carlene Kyeremeh, Vice-President of Academic and Student Affairs at All Nations University in Ghana, observes (ACU, n.d.),

> *What many think is online teaching is not online teaching. It isn't just uploading the course material .... We must be able to ensure students are consistently engaging with the content and activities. PEBL has been a great source of guidance on this.*

Designing online courses is a challenge in its own right, and delivering them is another, especially in environments where staff are already stretched thin managing with limited resources.

PEBL's current outreach is bringing together universities in Nigeria and Ghana with international partners, including the University of New South Wales, Australia, who can provide expertise in creating quality-assured and credit-bearing courses that can be shared across the region. PEBL has already brought on board 23 universities in East Africa (ACU, n.d.), partnering them with colleagues from the UK and Canada, reaching 11,000 students and training more than 170 academics in creating quality-assured open-source modules. Six were added to OER Africa in 2016, and a further nine added in 2019 (Hu, 2020). Perhaps even more important than creating these starting assets, PEBL has trained staff and collaborated with West African universities, sharing experience as they begin to design their blended learning programmes, which they will thenceforth be able to deliver with full independence.

Again, an obvious challenge for blended learning is the unequal availability of Internet access outlined earlier in this chapter. The ACU has called upon policy-makers to rectify this digital divide by prioritizing funding, bringing together universities, students, global employers, and telecommunications companies to agree on a common agenda on digital education that can be worked towards and providing a platform for digital educators to discuss common challenges and compare experiences so that those further along the digital journey can share their discoveries with colleagues earlier in the process (ACU, 2020). Meanwhile, some PEBL universities have also negotiated data packages with companies so that students are able to access free internet (Hu, 2020).

Universities and students still face difficulties in implementing and accessing digital teaching, and ACU continues to innovate and advocate to support the education community in overcoming them. However, if these challenges can be overcome, blended learning presents an opportunity for universities to quickly and sustainably increase their capacity to reach students and develop a truly diverse and well-informed population.

CIRCLE and PEBL are two successful examples of ACU's collaborative outreach, but there are a host of others, both already in execution and in preparation. Through the established networks of the Commonwealth, ACU's collaboration with the international community enables universities to deliver new forms of teaching and community outreach that maximize both the practical and the intellectual resources of under-served regions.

University networks are already showing their value as vital nexuses for the sharing of best practice and scientific knowledge, and the ACU has worked with institutions to create several. The Higher Education and SDGs Network (ACU, n.d.) agenda focuses on creating sustainable goals for university operations, sharing SDG-related research, and co-creating projects for impact and community engagement to bring these goals to reality. The Commonwealth Peace and Reconciliation Network (ACU, n.d.) brings together academics and university staff from across multiple disciplines to facilitate honest and constructive dialogue about justice and reconciliation in the face of colonial legacies. The HR in HE Community is a forum for experienced HR professionals to share strategies for developing the HR functioning within their institutions (ACU, n.d.). The Supporting Research Community connects ACU member universities to share challenges and ideas for supporting the research process, from administration and library services to impact and uptake (ACU, n.d.). Finally, the Commonwealth Climate Resilience Network (CCRN), partnered with Fiji National University, the University of the South Pacific, and the University of the West Indies, provides a channel through which universities in regions directly hit by climate change can exchange expertise with universities with specialist research in building resilience and disaster preparedness.

To discuss the CCRN in a little more detail: it is a body through which researchers can connect with each other as well as policymakers, providing opportunities both for new collaborations and direct advocacy (ACU, n.d.). The CCRN awards grants to member universities to fund work aimed at enhancing resilience either in the universities themselves, or in communities, businesses, and governments (ACU, n.d.). The grants can be used for a wide range of initiatives, from improving teaching of climate change adaptation to developing tools to make universities more prepared to continue their work in worst-case scenarios. Recent funded initiatives include: a project to develop a model of Fiji's sea surface temperature and its effect on marine life, creating an early warning system that can be shared with other island States with comparable ecosystems; the development of a postgraduate certificate in Climate Change Vulnerability Assessment at the University of Saskatchewan, Canada; a climate change product developed at the University of the West Indies that will improve the understanding and preparedness of primary school children; and a series of workshops created by the University of Venda, South Africa, aiming to train 500 young social and environmental entrepreneurs among students and community youth.

The wide reach of the CCRN allows for academics not only to work on vital projects with proper funding but also to connect with colleagues working in similar disciplines but in different cultural and environmental contexts, allowing for an interchange of ideas leading to a stronger academic and advocacy platform that any could achieve in isolation.

The ambitions of the SDGs are not small: a global change will be necessary if the planet is to be safeguarded. By bringing universities and other stakeholders together in pursuit of shared solutions, the ACU is preparing for the inescapable challenges of the future. For everyone's sake, the resources of better-funded universities and the expertise of those on the front lines must be shared. No single issue, from climate change to poverty, happens in a vacuum: each contributes to the other, and so must the solutions. For a nation to be stable and prosperous, it needs an educated population, and to face the future with hope, it needs the best scientific and community preparation. Without these, the SDGs are unlikely to be achieved, but with collaboration, there is hope for all of us.

REFERENCES

2nd International RESUP Conference: Inequalities in Higher Education and Research. (2009). Study Network on Higher Education (RESUP). https://calenda.org/212021?file=1

21st Conference of Commonwealth Education Ministers Ministerial Statement: "Rethinking Education for Innovation, Growth and Sustainability post-Covid-19". (2022, April). https://bit.ly/3daMYQ0

A National Education Opportunities Network (UK) World Access to Higher Education Day (WAHED). (2021). *Perspectives on the challenges to access and equity in Higher Education across the world in the context of COVID*. World Access to Higher Education Network. https://worldaccesshe.com/wp-content/uploads/2021/09/SBT2369-National-Education-Opportunities-Network-NEON-Report-Design-v3-Single-Page.pdf

Action Groups. (n.d.). *Commonwealth*. https://thecommonwealth.org/bluecharter/action-groups

Blueprint for SDG Leadership. (n.d.). *UN global compact*. https://www.unglobalcompact.org/take-action/action/sdg-blueprint

CIRCLE. (n.d.). ACU. https://www.acu.ac.uk/get-involved/circle/

Commonwealth Blue Charter. (n.d.). *Commonwealth*. https://thecommonwealth.org/bluecharter

Commonwealth Charter. (n.d.). *Commonwealth*. https://thecommonwealth.org/charter

Commonwealth Climate Resilience Challenge Grants. (n.d.). ACU. https://www.acu.ac.uk/funding-opportunities/for-university-staff/grants/commonwealth-climate-resilience-challenge-grants/

Commonwealth Climate Resilience Network. (n.d.). ACU. https://www.acu.ac.uk/get-involved/commonwealth-climate-resilience-network/

Commonwealth Peace and Reconciliation Network. (n.d.). ACU. https://www.acu.ac.uk/get-involved/commonwealth-peace-and-reconciliation-network/

Commonwealth Scholarship Commission in the UK. (n.d.). https://cscuk.fcdo.gov.uk/

Da Wan, C. (2021, April 26). *Captive minds*. ACU. https://www.acu.ac.uk/the-acu-review/captive-minds/

Education. (2020, July 23). *United Nations sustainable development*. https://www.un.org/sustainabledevelopment/education/

Gender Grants. (n.d.). ACU. https://www.acu.ac.uk/funding-opportunities/for-university-staff/grants/gender-grants/

Higher Education and the SDGs Network. (n.d.). ACU. https://www.acu.ac.uk/get-involved/higher-education-and-the-sdgs-network/

HR in HE Community. (n.d.). ACU. https://www.acu.ac.uk/get-involved/hr-in-he-community/

Hu, D. (2020, September 7). Optimising virtual learning beyond *Covid*-19. The Association of Commonwealth Universities. https://www.acu.ac.uk/news/optimising-virtual-learning/

Kelly, E., Doyle, V., & Kelly, M. (2021, July). *Evaluation report – Independent review: Institutional capacity strengthening of Climate Impacts Research Capacity and Leadership Enhancement (CIRCLE).* https://www.acu.ac.uk/media/3455/circle-institutional-capacity-review-evaluation-report-final.pdf

Kromydas, T. (2017). Rethinking higher education and its relationship with social inequalities: Past knowledge, present state and future potential. *Palgrave Communications*, *3*, 1. https://doi.org/10.1057/s41599-017-0001-8

Newman, J. (2022a, March 31). The Turing scheme: New horizons for international student mobility. *Industry Insight from Professionals in International Education*. https://blog.thepienews.com/2022/03/the-turing-scheme-new-horizons-for-international-student-mobility/

Newman, J. (2022b, June 4). *How to help researchers make the connections that matter*. University World News. https://www.universityworldnews.com/post.php?story=20220530113218755

Newman, J. (2022c, July 1). *Blended learning is the key to boosting the participation in Africa*. Times Higher Education. https://www.timeshighereducation.com/blog/blended-learning-key-boosting-he-participation-africa

Partnership for enhanced and blended learning (PEBL). (n.d.). ACU. https://www.acu.ac.uk/get-involved/pebl/pebl-east-africa/

PEBL West Africa. (n.d.). ACU. https://www.acu.ac.uk/get-involved/pebl/pebl-west-africa/

Queen Elizabeth Commonwealth Scholarships. (n.d.). ACU. https://www.acu.ac.uk/funding-opportunities/for-students/scholarships/queen-elizabeth-commonwealth-scholarships/

Research showcase: Blue Charter Fellowships 2019–20. (n.d.). https://www.acu.ac.uk/get-involved/blue-charter-2019-2020-research-showcase/

Scholarships. (n.d.). ACU. https://www.acu.ac.uk/funding-opportunities/for-students/scholarships/

Skopec, M., Issa, H., Reed, J., & Harris, M. (2020). The role of geographic bias in knowledge diffusion: A systematic review and narrative synthesis. *Research Integrity and Peer Review*, *5*, 2. https://doi.org/10.1186/s41073-019-0088-0

Stories of Change. (n.d.). ACU. https://www.acu.ac.uk/get-involved/stories-of-change/developing-women-leaders-in-research/

Supporting Research Community. (n.d.). ACU. https://www.acu.ac.uk/get-involved/supporting-research-community/

The Association of Commonwealth Universities. (2015). Progress and potential – acu.ac.uk. (2015). https://www.acu.ac.uk/media/2181/progress_and_potential_higher_education_playing_its_part_in_the_sustainable_development_goals.pdf

The Association of Commonwealth Universities (ACU). (2020a). *Higher education during COVID-19: A snapshot of digital engagement in commonwealth universities*. ACU. https://www.acu.ac.uk/media/2344/acu-policy-brief-digital-engagement-2020.pdf

The Association of Commonwealth Universities (ACU). (2020b). *Higher education during COVID-19: A snapshot of digital engagement in commonwealth universities. Detailed results and analysis*. ACU. https://www.acu.ac.uk/media/2345/acu-digital-engagement-survey-detailed-results.pdf

The Association of Commonwealth Universities (ACU). (2020c, September 1). *Higher education during COVID-19: A snapshot of digital engagement in Commonwealth Universities*. ACU. https://www.acu.ac.uk/news/higher-education-during-covid-19-a-snapshot-of-digital-engagement-in-commonwealth-universities/

The Association of Commonwealth Universities (ACU). (2021). *The road to 2030: Building a better world through higher education*. ACU. https://www.acu.ac.uk/media/3828/acu-strategy-the-road-to-2030.pdf

The Association of Commonwealth Universities (ACU). (2022a, January 12). *ACU and British Council publish report evidencing how international higher education partnerships contribute to all 17 SDGs*. ACU. https://www.acu.ac.uk/news/international-higher-education-partnerships-report/

The Association of Commonwealth Universities (ACU). (2022b, June 20). *ACU launches PEBL West Africa at CHOGM 2022*. ACU. https://www.acu.ac.uk/news/acu-launches-pebl-west-africa-at-chogm-2022/

The Association of Commonwealth Universities (ACU). (2022c, August 18). *Commonwealth students unite to harness the power of sport at ACU summer school 2022*. ACU. https://www.acu.ac.uk/news/commonwealth-students-unite-to-harness-the-power-of-sport-at-acu-summer-school-2022/

The Association of Commonwealth Universities (ACU). (n.d.-a). *Commonwealth higher education Stakeholder Group's submission to The Conference of Commonwealth Education Ministers*. ACU. https://www.acu.ac.uk/media/4161/acu-21ccem-commonwealth-higher-education-stakeholder-reccomendations.pdf

The Association of Commonwealth Universities (ACU). (n.d.-b). *Our history*. ACU. https://www.acu.ac.uk/about-us/our-history/

The Association of Commonwealth Universities (ACU). (n.d.-c). *The Internationalist: Episode three transcript – Belonging at university, an equal future?* ACU. https://www.acu.ac.uk/media/2599/episode-three-transcript.pdf

The Commonwealth. (2022, June 25). *Commonwealth adopts historic living lands charter*. Commonwealth. https://thecommonwealth.org/news/commonwealth-adopts-historic-living-lands-charter

Time for a World Education Service: Focused, Free and for All. (n.d.). Institute for Global Change. https://institute.global/policy/time-world-education-service-focused-free-and-all

United Nations. (2015). *Taking stock of the global partnership for development*. https://www.un.org/millenniumgoals/pdf/MDG_Gap_2015_E_web.pdf

United Nations. (n.d.-a). *Goal 4*. Department of Economic and Social Affairs. United Nations. https://sdgs.un.org/goals/goal4

United Nations. (n.d.-b). *Sustainable development goals (SDGs)*. UN Office for Sustainable Development. United Nations. https://unosd.un.org/content/sustainable-development-goals-sdgs

5

RETHINKING PARTNERSHIPS IN OUR LIVED SPACES: A KEY TO ACHIEVING THE SDGs

Susan T. L. Harrison and Maano Ramutsindela

ABSTRACT

A rich and productive history of collaborative research has given the University of Cape Town (UCT) many opportunities to observe the traditional workings of research partnerships across all levels – and to recognise how new models of collaboration might better address the United Nations' (UN) Sustainable Development Goals (SDGs). Human needs are intertwined with a healthy environment and require specific policy interventions by various actors. Responses to COVID-19 demonstrated the significance of such interventions. The African Union's Agenda 2063: The Africa We Want (which is aligned to achieving the SDGs in Africa) notes the interrelated factors that can often only be analysed effectively through interdisciplinary approaches. In this chapter, the authors use case studies to argue that the minimum requirements for achieving the SDGs are: rethinking partnerships that support the socioecological systems on which life and the future of both humanity and the planet depend; adopting an approach that informs the management and governance of specific geographic areas and how the world and its millions of different communities work together to achieve those goals; and cultivating partnerships that are 'Global South friendly' with the objective of creating equitable societies at a global scale.

Keywords: Collaboration; intersectionality; human condition; interdisciplinarity; partnership; equity

INTRODUCTION

As aptly expressed by the late Kofi Annan when he served as Secretary General of the UN, 'Our biggest challenge in this century is to take an idea that seems abstract – sustainable development – and turn it into a reality for all the world's people' (MacAskill, 2001, quoting Kofi Annan).

Partnership is key to global sustainable development. SDG17 challenges us to reassess models and forms of partnerships that have been used during many years of addressing development challenges at national, regional, and global levels (United Nations Department of Economic and Social Affairs (UN DESA). It invites us to refine and promote partnerships that have delivered tangible results while also seeking to develop new models for collaboration, with the goal of building a sustainable approach to life on our planet. Countries in the Global South in general, and Africa in particular, have many and varied experiences of partnerships for development, and have served as testing grounds for ideas of development inspired by economic ideologies and models. These have had mixed results. For example, structural adjustment programmes, introduced by Global North organisations such as the World Bank and the International Monetary Fund, imposed stringent economic policies on nations that already had a high level of poverty. Instead of strengthening these economies, the programmes only increased the burden carried by vulnerable groups such as women and children. In these ways, they have had devasting effects on societies in the Global South[1] (Mkandawire & Soludo, 1998).

Given these experiences, what forms of partnerships should we forge to achieve the SDGs? What should be the ethical foundations for these partnerships? And how do we manage the power dynamics associated with inequalities and injustices?

The concept of sustainable development can only be realised through its translation from theory to action, via idea generation, theorising, and implementation. This requires diverse and intersectoral partnerships that prioritise human needs, environmental health, and economic well-being. Sustainable development must recognise intersecting relationships: for example, climate adaptation intersects with access to water, food security, building healthy environments, and education. Further, we need to target this interdisciplinary knowledge built on strong disciplines, focusing on both discrete SDGs and their relationship to each other. In this way research partnerships will make a meaningful impact on policy decisions, actions within community networks, civic society, government, and the business sector. The SDGs cannot be addressed in silos. They require collaborative, targeted, engaged, and action-oriented partnership.

Sustainable development requires a focus on social justice. In our institutional strategic plan titled Vision 2030, the UCT defines social justice as the redressing of inequality 'through the work we do – whether in teaching, research or service in partnership with communities – because it is also about redressing inequality in broader societies on the continent' (Haw, 2020). In this context, true progress towards delivery of the SDGs is not feasible without a focus on just and equitable partnerships. An unjust world is not sustainable; building towards an equitable future needs to be centre stage.

Accelerating the pace and scale of achieving the SDGs in Africa requires a step-change. In response, UCT has embarked on a path of collaborative research, building complex partnerships beyond the limited scope of conventional academic partnerships while also leveraging them. In this way, we are driving towards an equitable future that will maintain a sustainable planet by guiding the intersection of the work of communities, civic society, government, NGOs, academic institutions, religious and secular organisations, and business.

In this chapter, we recount examples of a rich and productive history of collaborative research that has given UCT many opportunities to observe the traditional workings of partnerships across all levels – and to strive for new models of collaboration that are required for achieving the SDGs. Such models allow us to focus on specific SDG themes as well as to work across spaces where human needs are intersectional. They recognise how human needs depend on a healthy environment. They apply an approach that takes into account the many wicked problems we all share on a global scale.

We present selected case studies from our university that are helping to advance the SDGs and a sustainable, equitable, fair, and just society, with a focus on the operating environment of the Global South. We identify the major challenges experienced in advancing the SDGs and the solutions formulated to exponentially accelerate work on the SDGs in UCT's respective research areas. We also discuss how these examples of research partnerships can advance global education for sustainable development as promoted by UNESCO (2020) and in support of SDG4: 'Ensure inclusive and equitable quality education and promote lifelong learning opportunities for all' (UN DESA).

The case studies presented here include work on the SDGs in Africa, the African chapter of the Intergovernmental Panel on Climate Change (IPCC), community-based interventions in cancer, transdisciplinary programme in mining science and policy, and rapid responses to COVID-19.

BUILDING NETWORKS OF FOCUSED RESEARCH TOWARDS DELIVERY OF THE AFRICAN UNION'S AGENDA 2063 AND THE UN'S SDGs IN AFRICA

UCT capitalised on its membership in the Worldwide University Network (WUN) to co-lead, with the University of Western Australia, the formation of the Global Africa Group (GAG) within the network in 2015. At the time, the 23-member international research university network sought to foster research collaborations across continents focusing on four global challenges: higher education and research, public health (non-communicable disease), climate change, and understanding cultures. The GAG emerged as a cross-cutting, regionally focused collaboration of WUN members whose research areas are relevant to Africa's research and development agendas, are linked to international debates and scholarship, and involve dynamic and equal partnerships between the African and non-African university members of the WUN in setting research priorities and in co-designing and co-producing research projects (Ramutsindela & Mickler, 2020).

The GAG conceptualised a research project on SDG17: 'Strengthen the means of implementation and revitalise the global partnership for development'. It focused on the need to

> *enhance the global partnership for sustainable development, complemented by multi-stakeholder partnerships that mobilise and share knowledge, expertise, technology and financial resources, to support the achievement of the sustainable development goals in all countries, particularly developing countries. (UN DESA)*

Partnerships raise key questions of inclusion and legitimacy, and the consequent economic, environmental, political, and social outcomes (Ponte et al., 2022).

The GAG project grappled with how to create equitable partnerships and collaborations in a higher education and research sector characterised by inequalities; how to counter structural conditions that inhibit the co-production of knowledge for the SDGs; how to work at the intersection of African and global development debates and agendas; how to provide a platform for engaging in critical thinking on theoretical frameworks and questions that shape 'Global-Africa' discourses, debates, and policies; and how to bring existing knowledge in various fields and experiences into the service of SDGs. To answer these questions, the GAG developed a methodology for collaborative research that culminated in an edited volume, *Africa and the Sustainable Development Goals* (Ramutsindela & Mickler, 2020).

Two main lessons came from the project. The first is that equality in partnerships for achieving SDGs requires a rigorous methodology underpinned by well-defined principles. To counter the marginalisation of African knowledge and experience in global scholarship, the GAG had to think carefully about the co-production of knowledge, the inclusion of Africa-based ideas and priorities, and the affirmation of knowledge produced by scholars based on the continent. The group developed a principle of co-authorship that required each chapter of the book to be co-conceived and co-authored with at least one of the co-authors based at a university on the African continent.

The second lesson is that much of the knowledge required for the SDGs in their various contexts is already available but requires partnerships to harness it. Therefore, the GAG project developed three broad themes to which collaborators contributed from the work they had already done outside the SDG framing. The themes were: 'Africa's sustainable development: approaches, institutions, agendas'; 'Scientific evidence and critical thinking on the SDGs in Africa'; and 'Africa and the SDGs: the role of collaborative research'. Eighty-one individual collaborators from five continents used results from previous and ongoing research to speak to the SDGs in relation to challenges the continent faces and the solutions that governments, practitioners, donors, and ordinary people should consider. Though this project focused on Africa's development priorities, it highlighted the needs and aspirations that are central to the implementation of the SDGs.

EXPANDING A BINATIONAL ACADEMIC PARTNERSHIP TO INFORM POLICY AT NATIONAL GOVERNMENT LEVEL ACROSS AFRICA AND THE GLOBAL SOUTH

Climate Adaptation and Resilience (CLARE) is a Canada–UK partnership to enable socially inclusive and sustainable action to build resilience to climate change and natural hazards for people across the Global South (IRDC, 2022). The African Climate and Development Initiative (ACDI) at UCT has led the African activity on this partnership to increase the uptake of Africa-focused climate change impacts and adaptation research within the UN's IPCC Working Group II assessment process and to directly inform multiple policy processes.

Through synthesis research that brought together large amounts of existing data and knowledge on climate resilient development in Africa, the project influenced understanding of climate change risk across the entire IPCC 6th Assessment Report and directly informed multiple policy processes. Actors in planning, programme implementation, policy, and research used a range of evidence-based options to enhance and support communities' livelihoods in the face of climate challenges, in ways that benefit the most vulnerable Africans.

In this way the project supported SDG13 ('Take Urgent Action to Combat Climate Change and Its Impacts') and SDG15 ('Protect, Restore, and Promote Sustainable Use of Terrestrial Ecosystems') by increasing the capacity of researchers and networks across Africa, advising on government policy, and highlighting the need for increased education and public awareness of climate change among Africans (UN DESA).

ACDI successfully completed the 'Africa Chapter' (Chapter 9) and 'Decision-making Options for Managing Risk' (Chapter 17) of the IPCC Working Group II Contribution to the Sixth Assessment Report. The high level of data and knowledge integration in the Africa chapter elevated it into a position of thought leadership in the IPCC Working Group II Summary for Policymakers.

Chapter authors led sections of the Summary for Policymakers on climate finance, complex climate change risk, solar geoengineering, climate change literacy, and observed climate change impacts. The ACDI also produced a series of fact sheets on the IPCC key findings for the southern, central, western, eastern, and northern regions of Africa, in English, French, and Portuguese, in collaboration with the Climate and Development Knowledge Network. They have been shared in multiple science policy forums.

The work of the ACDI yielded a library of Africa-focused documents for policy-makers and other academics, as demonstrated in Table 5.1.

HEALTH INTERVENTIONS WITH IMPACT: MATCHING KNOWLEDGE WITH EFFECTIVE TRANSLATION IN THE COMMUNITY TO TREAT CERVICAL CANCER

The UCT Department of Obstetrics and Gynaecology launched the Khayelitsha Cervical Cancer Screening Project (KCCSP) in 1995, in collaboration with Columbia University in New York, as a community-based health research project to identify a novel approach to cervical cancer prevention in low-resource settings.

Table 5.1. Reports Produced or Supported by the ACDI/CLARE Project.[a]

The first Africa-wide assessments of: the feasibility and effectiveness of climate change adaptation actions; and climate change literacy rates, highlighting the fact that women have lower climate change literacy rates than men and the importance of increasing secondary and tertiary education to help address this gap
Africa-wide assessment of climate change research funding since 1990, revealing how less than 4% of that funding has focused on Africa (most goes to institutions in the EU, UK, and USA), and only around 1% of funding has gone directly to researchers in Africa
The African Union (AU) Climate Change and Resilient Development Strategy and Action Plan, 2022–2032
African Group of Negotiators Expert Support (AGNES) Common Position on Enhanced Climate Action on Land. A briefing note for a common position for African negotiators
Summary for Urban Policymakers. Setting the research agenda for a future IPCC Special Report on Cities and Settlements by the Sea proposed for the IPCC 7th Assessment Cycle
International Council on Monuments and Sites (ICOMOS) White Paper on Climate Change and Heritage
Understanding Complex Climate Change Risks. An updated risk framework that has since been used by Belgium's Federal Minister for Climate, Environment, Sustainable Development and Green Deal and by the USA Department of Energy in establishing their own respective risk assessments
Shaping the Future of Mobility in Africa: Addressing Climate-Forced Displacement & Migration, an Africa Climate Mobility Initiative to be released at COP27
IPCC Synthesis Report Authorship. The most important findings from the three IPCC Special Reports and the three IPCC Working Group Reports published since 2018, to be published in March 2023
Adaptation Futures 2023. How the findings of the IPCC reports can influence Africa's Adaptation priorities
The results of the work were presented to the South African public in a SAPCC *Dialogue on Climate Resilient Development Pathways* on 15 August 2022 (Climate Commission, 2022)
UN Environment Programme: An advisory brief for the UN Secretary General on solar geoengineering, and potential positions the UN could take on the topic of geoengineering

[a] References for the IPCC project: the IPCC chapter on Africa: https://www.ipcc.ch/report/ar6/wg2/downloads/report/IPCC_AR6_WGII_Chapter09.pdf; the IPCC chapter on decision-making: https://www.ipcc.ch/report/ar6/wg2/downloads/report/IPCC_AR6_WGII_Chapter17.pdf; and the ACDI/CLARE Project factsheets: https://cdkn.org/ar6-africa

The focus of the KCCSP has been the prevention of cervical cancer through screening women for precancerous lesions of the cervix. Historically this was done by performing Pap smears on women in national cervical cancer control programmes. However, the infrastructure, human resources, and other costs have proven to be prohibitively expensive for developing countries with fragile health systems. As a consequence, more than 85% of cases of cervical cancer and nearly 90% of all cervical cancer deaths occur in developing countries.

In South Africa, about 10,000 women a year are diagnosed with cervical cancer, of whom more than 5,000 will die from the disease. Most of these cases are found in black South African women, who rely on under-funded and inadequate public health care. Even then, access is often hampered by travel costs to treatment centres and inaccessibility for those in unforgiving work environments.

Through years of research and testing, KCCSP staff found a simpler alternative to Pap smears in the form of modern human papillomavirus (HPV) testing, which is also more accurate in detecting precancerous lesions than Pap smears. Patients can be screened for HPV and treated in the same visit. Following the screening session, women are provided with refreshments and educational materials while results are processed, allowing the follow-on treatment to be performed within an hour.

The default rate (i.e. percentage of patients who do not present for treatment following a positive diagnosis through abnormal Pap smear) among patients at the KCCSP is less than 10%, comparing favourably to the hospital colposcopy clinic at which recorded default rates of women with abnormal Pap smears are between 40% and 60%. Combining a patient-centred approach, the empowerment of women through knowledge, providing services near to their homes, and listening to and acting upon their health needs has proven to be an effective approach. The work of the KCCSP has been duplicated in many countries in sub-Saharan Africa, Asia, and Latin America, and the KCCSP contributed towards the introduction of national HPV vaccination in South Africa.

The KCCSP has also uplifted the skills of clinicians and researchers across Africa (Metelerkamp, 2022).

Most of the women who have benefitted directly from the work of the KCCSP live in Khayelitsha, an informal settlement in Cape Town with high levels of poverty. Many South African women are not comfortable discussing the reproductive system and genital area. The Project Director, Professor Lynette Denny of UCT, worked with traditional healers and a praise singer to help women in Khayelitsha to become more comfortable and even proud of these parts of their bodies. The praise singer wrote a poem declared that even Nelson Mandela was born through the vagina. The KCCSP team members sang that song in the streets of the township to encourage women to be proud of their bodies (Huisman, 2021).

Professor Denny has written more than 130 peer-reviewed research papers sharing the innovations and findings of the KCCSP, while her staff and students have published an additional 30 articles. Three PhD candidates completed their degrees, and an additional PhD candidate is in progress.

Denny has trained 12 registered nurses to perform visual inspection of the cervix; diagnose and treat sexually transmitted disease; diagnose and refer women with pathology of the vulva; treat precancerous lesions of the cervix with cryotherapy and, more recently, thermocoagulation; record a gynecologically relevant clinical history; and to triage and refer women for more specialised evaluation. They receive good clinical practice training and research methods, ethics, and implementation, with training reviews every four months.

The KCCSP has trained approximately 10 doctors to perform colposcopies and to function as non-surgical gynaecologists; to follow good clinical practice, research methodology, and research ethics; to adhere to regulatory requirements; and to manage non-research-related clinical problems. These doctors were co-authors on scientific publications and participated in the preparation of manuscripts.

The KCCSP has also trained close to 30 community health workers as formal translators and educators of patients. They learned how to administer questionnaires and to engage with patients in a respectful, dignified manner; to understand problems of women and which patients to refer to the doctors and nursing sisters; to ensure excellent adherence by the patients to the project protocols; and to do home visits or telephone tracking. Most were also trained in how to be a clinical assistant to the doctor. Three data capturers were also trained during the course of the project.

The work of the KCCSP has been praised not only by provincial healthcare leaders but also by South African President Cyril Ramaphosa, who awarded Professor Denny with the national Order of the Baobab (Silver) in November 2021, in recognition not only of her research and medical practice but also her contributions towards building a non-racial, non-sexist, democratic, and prosperous South Africa.

CROSSING THE STAKEHOLDER SPECTRUM: THE ROLE OF ACADEMIA, COMMUNITY, NGOs, AND INDUSTRY IN DRIVING TOWARDS SUSTAINABLE DEVELOPMENT THROUGH MINERAL EXTRACTION

For over a century in Africa, mining was viewed solely as an extractive business, with little consideration for environmental protection or the well-being of the surrounding communities or indigenous people. More recently, mining in Africa has changed from simply balancing production targets with cost control to a complex set of interrelationships including safety, health, the environment, sustainable development, and, increasingly, proactive stakeholder management. Mineral extraction now needs to contribute towards building robust and resilient communities around the source of the extraction, through integrated partnerships of industry, government, and community.

A transdisciplinary and inter-institutional Master of Philosophy (MPhil) Degree programme, offered through the Minerals to Metals Research Initiative in the Department of Chemical Engineering at UCT, with an intercalated sister Master of Science programme offered by the University of Zambia (UNZA) on a decentralised basis, has aimed to educate and train graduates who can:

- Bring to the programme knowledge and experience from across the mining sector in southern Africa and beyond.

- Develop deep disciplinary knowledge at an advanced level in and around the African mining industry.
- Integrate this disciplinary knowledge of multiple players into interdisciplinary approaches, bringing together anthropology, sociology, economics, law, environmental scientists, engineers, health practitioners, and other disciplines and partner these disciplines with the knowledge and experience of academia, government, industry, the NGO sector, and community stakeholders to inform approaches to the mine planning, technology implemented, environmental management, community building, resource efficiency, economic value, and so forth.
- Combine that knowledge with a broader understanding of the complex sustainable challenges facing industry and society.
- Work with various stakeholders through integration of the needs of community, environment, government, and industry, exercising sensitivity on how to project this knowledge in the context of different stakeholders.

Teaching and research within the programme explore ways to:

- Impart a high-level understanding of, and a sensitivity and progressive approach to, the critical factors of sustainable development in the context of mining and minerals processing in Africa and their respective communities.
- Respect the interrelationships between safety, health, the environment, economic development, and proactive stakeholder management, and the concomitant integration of technical skills, ethics, and global citizenship.
- Recognise the need for long-term resilient communities to outlive the mine without paying the long-term environmental costs of the mining operation.
- Promote experimentation with interdisciplinary and systemic approaches to environmental protection and socioeconomic development in the context of geo-extractive industries in Africa.

This programme trains fresh graduates, those in mid-term career positions and leaders of the industry and community, side by side, in principles and practices that support the global SDGs, including SDG6 (Clean Water and Sanitation), SDG8 (Decent Work and Economic Growth), SDG9 (Industry, Innovation and Infrastructure), SDG11 (Sustainable Cities and Communities), SDG12 (Sustainable Consumption and Production), and SDG15 (Life on Land) (UN DESA). Underlying themes of the programme are bridging the gap between science and policy, capitalising on convening power, and creating new perspectives on real issues and challenges faced by modern mining.

The research philosophy of the programme involves a holistic approach to mining that prioritises the integration of people, plants, and prosperity, as illustrated in Fig. 5.1.

This two-year MPhil Degree was initiated in 2014 in tandem with the MSc degree at the UNZA. Field sites have spanned the South African and Zambian mining sectors. So far, the MPhil programme run through UCT has 20 graduates who came from five different African countries, Australia, and Japan, while

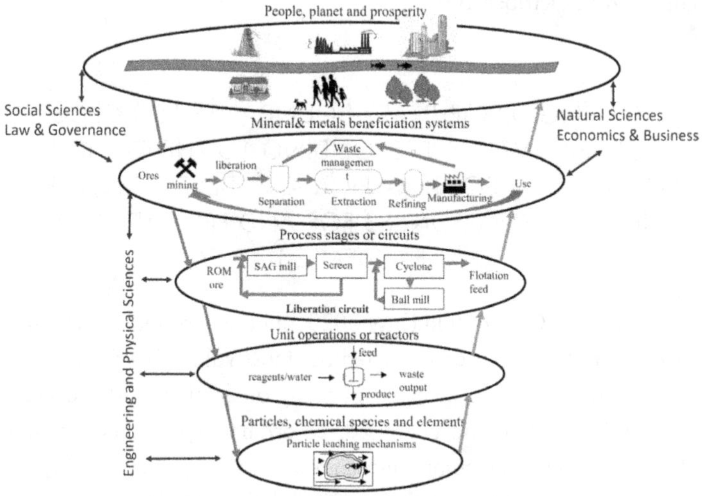

Compiled by Jennifer Broadhurst, Minerals to Metals, University of Cape Town, South Africa.

Fig. 5.1. Research Philosophy Towards Responsible Mining: The Five-tiered Approach.

105 Zambian students took part in the master's programme run through UNZA. Their backgrounds span across 18 different disciplines covering the engineering, natural science, law, humanities, and health meta-disciplines. The UCT degree is accredited by the Higher Education Quality Committee of South Africa. Candidates are required to complete advanced study by coursework and a research dissertation.

The success of the programme is built on expanding partnerships to build diverse thinking, doing, and being. It created partnerships between academia, industry, environmental agents, and community stakeholders and between students from very different lived experience. As an example, the vice-president of a large mining company and the traditional chief from a mining community interacted as part of the same student cohort, enhancing the diverse fabric of experience and learnings, and, through their success in the programme, contributing to their very different environments of influence.

The programme was initiated by the Institute for Sustainability and Peace at the United Nations University through its programme on Education for Sustainable Development in Africa, which was launched in October 2008.

CROSSING DISCIPLINARY BOUNDARIES FOR CROSS-SECTORAL IMPACT: RESPONDING TO THE COVID-19 PANDEMIC IN SOUTH AFRICA AND DEVELOPING THE BRIEF FOR PREPAREDNESS FOR AND PREVENTION OF PANDEMICS

The onset of COVID-19 in early 2020 and the hard lock-down that followed in South Africa impacted the most vulnerable South Africans the most harshly, as it did in many other places. At the same time, it brought to life energised, co-ordinated partnerships that allowed the scientific community in South Africa to make a disproportionately effective contribution to global efforts in genomic surveillance, epidemiological modelling, immunology, and vaccinology.

Within a month of the first SARS-CoV-2 case detected in South Africa in March 2020, the National Department of Health established the South African COVID-19 Modelling Consortium: a group of local disease modellers, economists, clinicians, virologists, public health specialists, and researchers from academic, non-profit, and government institutions to provide, assess, and validate model-based evidence to support the planning needs of the government. Co-ordinated by the National Institute for Communicable Diseases (NICD), the consortium's core group of infectious disease and health economics modellers formed a partnership to produce models to project cases, deaths, and associated resource needs and health budget over the course of pandemic. Model-based evidence was regularly presented to the National COVID-19 Co-ordinating Council chaired by the country's President, the Ministerial Advisory Committees on COVID-19, the National Incident Management Team, the National Treasury and the Reserve Bank, as well as implementers and planners in various national and provincial government departments.

This partnership enabled funded support to provide COVID-19 modelling and budgeting support and expertise to other countries, thus boosting general pandemic preparedness. It established a communication pipeline for providing model-based evidence for routine national health planning.

With strong support from the South African Medical Research Council (SAMRC) and the Department of Science and Innovation (DSI), the South African National Variants Consortium was established in December 2020 as an informal grouping of biomedical and public health researchers across the country to define and address critical research questions relating to the Beta variant of SARS-CoV-2 initially. The needs-base enabled the free flow of information across universities, the SAMRC, DSI, National Health Laboratory Service (NHLS), NICD as well as research organisations. It removed the barriers that typically hinder co-operation across universities and between academic and public sectors, fully enabling rapid and deep science.

Positioned at the core of the consortium, the Network of Genomic Surveillance in South Africa brought together a network of NHLS laboratories with evolutionary biologists, virologists, and molecular epidemiologists. Working groups focused on surveillance and epidemiology, diagnostics, immunology, clinical, and vaccine research and collaborated to address priority questions. Weekly meetings allowed for rapid data processing and knowledge generation so that research outcomes could guide the national and global pandemic response. The informal, open, and flexible structure of the consortium also enabled participation by, and close collaboration with, healthcare providers from the private sector, thus illustrating the power of true public–private–academic partnership. Further, it demonstrated the potential for extending the Preparedness for and Prevention of Pandemics into the future.

FACILITATING PARTNERSHIP TO EMPOWER

The above case studies highlight critical aspects of partnership in expanding the SDGs across Africa. Countries across the Global South share many of the same broad challenges, including how they relate to research partnerships with colleagues in the Global North.

Cultivating partnerships that are Global South friendly is a necessary step in creating equitable societies in an equitable 'global village', including the Global North, where poverty and inequality are rapidly spreading, even in strong economies.

We have identified seven key principles of partnership for our South African environment.

- International partnerships often bring convening power, which facilitates and catalyses the initiatives that follow. This is demonstrated in the climate development case study, the sustainable development of mineral resources, and the community-based treatment of cervical cancer.
- Establishing equity in Global North: South partnerships is key to success. Too often well-intentioned North-led initiatives do not draw out the true issues of the Global South, as skewed power dynamics obstruct joint conceptualisation. Through development of strong and well-networked Global South partners and balanced partnerships, as demonstrated in the climate case study, the work of the Global South becomes seminal in defining global trends and the route forward. It is essential to

call out the imbalances in Global North:South partnerships to achieve effective equitable partnerships that deliver the desired outcomes for all.

- Intra-Africa partnerships have mobilised both the framing of continental climate development requirements and a continental response to the pandemic and future pandemic readiness. The Alliance of Research Universities in Africa (ARUA) and the African Union are already demonstrating their essential role as key players.
- Partnerships that cross-cut sectors and disciplines are an essential component of robust solutions to grand challenges – as shown in the case studies on the sustainable development of mineral resources and the pandemic. No matter how rigorous the regulations on behaviours, poor implementation through ineffective communication leads to inadequate understanding or buy-in that will limit or even negate benefits. Similarly, the successful treatment of cervical cancer is built through sensitive and empowering communication between knowledge creators and knowledge beneficiaries.
- Building engaged and socially responsive partnerships between academia and communities diversifies our learnings, often in ways that we least expect. It enables us to better understand the actual challenges and to unearth and mitigate polarised positions. The co-creation of effective solutions involves co-ownership and capacity development, as illustrated in the cervical cancer case study and, potentially, the case study on sustainable development of mineral resources.
- In positioning academic research to be relevant to the needs of the community or the nation, in engaging with governance structures, and in communicating beyond the academic literature, research contributes to policy and thus can have a global impact. This is demonstrated in the climate case study through the IPCC policy frameworks and in the sustainable development of mineral resources programme.
- Building a true community of action based on a driving need accelerates the impact and its expansion, as illustrated in the surveillance of COVID-19 in South Africa. The pandemic

positioned our relatively small scientific consortium to become a world leader in the rapid and expert identification and characterisation of new SARS-CoV-2 strains.

- Finally, building on the example above, the development of an academic-led modelling consortium provided key advice to government to inform decision-making throughout the pandemic. This example illustrates the extensive intellectual capacity housed in universities to which all governments have access. It highlights immense potential of the public–private–academic partnership and the social responsiveness role of universities to contribute to the solution of the world's wicked problems and the advance of the SDGs.

NOTE

1. Mkandawire and Soludo (1998). The World Bank March 2016 publication, *While Poverty in Africa Has Declined, Number of Poor Has Increased*, admits: "Poverty across the continent may be lower than what current estimates suggest, though the number of people living in extreme poverty has grown substantially since 1990, according to the latest World Bank Africa poverty report." Retrieved from https://www.worldbank.org/en/region/afr/publication/poverty-rising-africa-poverty-report

REFERENCES

Africa Union. (2023, February 19) *Agenda 2063: The Africa we want.* https://au.int/en/agenda2063/overview

Climate Commission. (2022, August 15). *Dialogue on climate resilient development pathways.* https://www.climatecommission.org.za/events/pcc-dialogue-on-climate-resilience-development-pathways-dialogue

Haw, P. (2020, August 24). *Vision 2030: Targeted strategies to redress inequality.* UCT. https://www.news.uct.ac.za/article/-2020-08-24-vision-2030-targeted-strategies-to-redress-inequality

Huisman, B. (2021). Prof Lynette Denny reflects on an extraordinary life of service. *Spotlight*, November 25. https://www.spotlightnsp.co.za/2021/11/25/face-to-face-prof-lynette-denny-reflects-on-an-extraordinary-life-of-service/

IRDC. (2022, August 8). *Enhanced finance, data and inclusion can help breach Africa's climate change adaptation gaps*. IRDC. https://www.idrc.ca/en/research-in-action/enhanced-finance-data-and-inclusion-can-help-breach-africas-climate-change

MacAskill, E. (2001). Annan pleads with west as environment is pushed up UN agenda. *The Guardian*, March 15. https://www.theguardian.com/environment/2001/mar/15/globalwarming.climatechange

Metelerkamp, T. (2022). Saving women – The powerful work of the Khayelitsha Cervical Cancer Screening Project. *Daily Maverick*, August 11. https://www.dailymaverick.co.za/article/2022-08-11-saving-women-the-powerful-work-of-the-khayelitsha-cervical-cancer-screening-project/

Mkandawire, P. T., & Soludo, C. C. (1998). *Our continent, our future: African perspectives on structural adjustment*. Council for the Development of Social Science Research in Africa.

Ponte, S., Noe, C., & Brockington, D. (Eds.). (2022). *Contested sustainability: The political ecology of conservation and development in Tanzania*. James Currey.

Ramutsindela, M., & Mickler, D. (Eds.). (2020). *Africa and the sustainable development goals*. SpringerLink.

UNESCO. (2020, July 20). ESD for 2030: What's next for education for sustainable development? UNESCO. https://en.unesco.org/news/esd-2030-whats-next-education-sustainable-development

United Nations Department of Economic and Social Affairs. (2023, February 19). *Sustainable Development*. https://sdgs.un.org/goals

6

THE POWER OF INTERGENERATIONAL PARTNERSHIP: STUDENTS, UNIVERSITIES, AND SDG17

Sam Vaghar, Summer Wyatt-Buchan, Shriya Dayal, Srijan Banik and Ayushi Nahar

ABSTRACT

Collaboration with student leaders is fundamental to the role of higher education in advancing the Sustainable Development Goals (SDG). In 2018, Millennium Campus Network (MCN) and the United Nations Academic Impact (UNAI) partnered to present the Millennium Fellowship. This semester-long leadership development program provides training, connections, and credentials to undergraduates advancing the SDGs. The Fellowship has rapidly expanded to draw over 25,000 applicants annually, with engagement on 136 campuses in 30 nations. This chapter unpacks how this program has grown through unique partnerships – with the United Nation (UN) and with universities. It also emphasizes best practices for how universities can support student leaders committed to the goals. Five best practices for collaboration will be shared:

1. *Break down silos* – Invite students to break out of their comfort zones, beyond campus, with discernment.
2. *Prioritize mentorship (1:1 and peer to peer)* – powerful faculty/staff–student relationships help students grow – and peer-to-peer mentorship builds robust communities of practice.
3. *Align incentives for collaboration* – from academic credit to seed funding, incentives can create an ideal environment for peer-to-peer collaboration.
4. *Build virtual community* – leverage technology to build cross-campus opportunities.
5. *Centre-student voice* – ensure students can co-create programs and opportunities.

To illuminate these points, we feature examples of Millennium Fellows' experiences in the program. The prevailing theme that emerges: building processes that centre-students' commitments and feedback builds trust and creates the foundation for dynamic partnerships to form.

Keywords: Student leadership; social impact; millennium Fellowship; sustainable development goals; SDG17; United Nations Academic Impact

With a 15-year track record working exclusively with university undergraduates across the globe to advance UN goals, the MCN has seen the power of partnerships firsthand. When students effectively collaborate with each other, with faculty and staff, with community leaders, and with more stakeholders, progress towards the SDGs is possible.

In this chapter, we outline our story and lessons from MCN and the Millennium Fellowship. We pay specific attention to the dynamics and mechanics of effective partnerships – told through our story and that of Millennium Fellows. We conclude with concrete, actionable recommendations for universities and stakeholders seeking to best support emerging leaders.

OUR FOUNDING IN DORM ROOMS

MCN was founded as a platform for undergraduates making a difference. Two books inspired MCN: *Mountains Beyond Mountains* about the late Dr Paul Farmer and Partners in Health, and *The End of Poverty* by Dr Jeffrey Sachs. Taken together, these books illuminated both pressing global injustices as well as concrete avenues to respond.

At 19, I (Sam) put down the books, picked up the phone, and cold-called and cold-emailed Professor Sachs. Two days later, I was at Columbia University meeting with his team. I shared, 'I am a sophomore at Brandeis. I know I don't have many answers yet, but I know we as students can do more to tackle extreme poverty'. I came back to campus, and we started small-scale public health fundraisers for bed nets to prevent malaria. In the fall of 2007, we convened student leaders from five area universities. There were shared challenges and aspirations. We asked, 'What would it look like to collaborate?' Anne Liu (MIT '08) shared that her team was planning a summit and she agreed to collaborate and call it the 'Millennium Campus Conference'. In April 2008, we hosted our inaugural summit at MIT. One thousand student leaders joined in, alongside Farmer, Sachs, John Legend, then-USAID Administrator Henrietta Fore, and more global leaders. Farmer, Legend, and Sachs joined our Board of Advisors, and MCN was formally launched.

EARLY GAPS AND FINDING ALIGNMENT

Our early summits at MIT, Columbia, and Harvard collectively drew thousands of undergraduate leaders. Our hypothesis was that this conference would create an ideal space to share best practices and form robust partnerships. We learned that we needed much more. Partnerships can be sparked at summits, but they often take longer to be built and sustained. We also found it difficult to meaningfully measure the impact of the summit. Without compelling data and alumni who quickly moved on after the events, we were failing to sustain long-term traction.

More than a decade later, I still remember conversations with our Board Members about what we might do. Will Herberich proposed the idea of a Fellowship, encouraging us to move beyond bright, shiny objects to explore how we might best support young leaders. We soon hired Abigail Ketchen, who designed a Fellowship curriculum from her experiences serving in the Peace Corps and drawing on 30 leadership curricula. When the Millennium Fellowship launched in Boston in 2013, it was extremely difficult to get students to respond. We had 15 applicants and 11 Millennium Fellows in that inaugural year.

That inaugural class helped us build trust. Our curriculum was tightly structured and tied to specific Key Performance Indicators to track our Fellows' organizations. Abigail centred students, mentoring and working closely to support their progress. As a result, the program gained traction, gradually growing year over year and expanding at universities in Boston, Miami, and New York City. A virtual edition coordinated by Raina Fox soon followed and enabled Millennium Fellows around the world to participate. Millennium Fellows like Netia McCray had innovative approaches to STEM education, while Felix Ruano helped volunteers with specific skills link up with organizations. Netia has taken her organization Mbadika full-time, while Felix has gone on to create a digital education platform for high school students, Subject.com.

As the Millennium Fellowship was refined year over year, we reflected on how we could best partner with and support undergraduates making a difference. As a small non-profit, we could not get every young leader an internship, job, or funding for their ventures. We dug deeper, seeking to get to the roots. How could we help young leaders build their own power to secure career pathways and support for their work? We identified three gaps in the market: training, connections, and credentials. Taken together, these three interventions provide Millennium Fellows with space to critically reflect, cultivate community, and build credibility for their emerging leadership.

In March 2017 I had a lunch meeting in New York City with the then-Chief of the UNAI, a network of over 1,500 academic institutions advancing UN goals. UNAI had a robust track record engaging with University Presidents, Vice-Chancellors, Deans, faculty, and staff. As we met, we shared our respective experiences in this space. UNAI had a strong network of academic institutions, and we complemented this with strong ties with undergraduate students. That lunch set in motion a process, several months long, to partner and present the Millennium Fellowship together. Each year, we would jointly invite undergraduate students from around the world to apply to the Millennium Fellowship by April. Selected Millennium Fellows would receive access to our core curriculum, reflecting in sessions on core elements of leadership and management in campus cohorts between August and November. These cohort sessions, along with virtual webinars, would give Fellows a network of support. Fellows would apply what they learned in real-time to projects advancing one or more of the SDGs in their communities. At the conclusion of the program, Fellows would earn a certificate of recognition from MCN and UNAI.

This model has driven the Millennium Fellowship's exponential growth. For the Class of 2019, there were 7,000 applicants. For the Class of 2022, there were 31,000 applicants from over 2,400 universities. The Fellowship now has active cohorts at 200 universities in 36 nations. Millennium Fellows collectively dedicate 250,000 hours to more than 1,000 grassroots initiatives, positively impacting the lives of more than 1.5 million people. The network is majority female and majority people of colour and this results in great diversity of Fellowship projects. At Alma College in the United States, Millennium Fellows created an aquaponics farm to tackle food insecurity on campus and in the local community. At the University of Benin in Nigeria, Fellows used solar power to provide electricity to 106 community members. At Al-Razi University in Yemen, Fellows are tackling malaria in a conflict region. And at multiple campuses, Fellows are working on grassroots campaigns to reduce stigma around mental health, advance sustainability locally, and support local artisans.

There are now more than 4,000 Millennium Fellowship Alumni. Among them 97% of Fellowship Alumni graduate from university and 87% of Fellowship alumni who are currently employed work in social impact careers. Behind these statistics are thousands of individual stories of young leaders leveraging MCN's core values – empathy, humility, and inclusion – to build robust partnerships. In the process, these young leaders have a rich collection of insights on the dynamics and mechanics of effective partnerships to advance the SDGs. Here are insights and reflections of recent

Millennium Fellowship Alumni from campuses in Bangladesh, India, and the UK.

SUMMER WYATT-BUCHAN

Millennium Fellow at University College London (UCL), UK, Class of 2021

Human Connection at the Heart of Partnerships

Next Chapter formed as part of the Millennium Fellowship Class of 2021 at UCL, where five UCL undergraduate students, from varying backgrounds, founded the project in London and Sicily. Next Chapter promotes migrants' integration through an educational program undertaken by middle and high school students in Italy, where students express their reflections through creating various artworks. The inspiration behind the project was the shared belief that forced migration to another country is not the end of the book but rather the beginning of a new chapter. The aim was to facilitate the integration of young refugees in both the British and Italian communities by combining two different perspectives. Italy is the arrival country for many refugees; therefore, it is imperative to recognize the connection between Italy and the UK, which acts as a secondary (or even tertiary) destination.

Since the founding of Next Chapter in November 2021, over 1,000 middle school and high school students have undertaken an educational program that explains the factors that intertwine within migration – topics such as prosecution, war, human rights, right of asylum, and daily life for refugee women and children. These students visited the Centro Astalli (the Italian section of the Jesuit Refugee Service) and met with a refugee who explained his migration journey through the Mediterranean route. After completing the educational program, students expressed their reflection through varying artistic means ranging from photography, to sculpture, to music, to letters, to videography. Marking the end of Next Chapters journey, UCL hosted a creative exhibition titled: *Different Human Perceptions of Migration*. People came to explore the artworks created by the Sicilian students and experience a snapshot of the journey that an unaccompanied minor took when undertaking the Mediterranean route of migration in 2017. The desired outcome of this exhibition was to break down stigmas surrounding forced migration and ultimately contribute to an inclusive society where refugees are welcome, safe, and are set up to thrive.

> *'Ciao cara amica, come va?'*
>
> *Hello Dear Friend, how are you?*
>
> *'Sarò sempre al tuo fianco non ti abbandonerò mai e vivremo assieme questa disavventura'*
>
> *I will always be by your side and I will never let you down. We will live this adventure together.*
>
> *– An extract taken from a letter addressed to a refugee child from a high school student*

The heart of 'Next Chapter' is human connection through partnerships between different countries, communities, organizations, and generations. The power of partnerships was clear from the beginning. Connected by the Millennium Fellowship and UCL, the first partnership within this project was student to student, all five from varying backgrounds, countries, and degrees specialisms and all connected through their passion for social impact and their commitment to the SDGs. The project's partnership grew to include various institutions, including UCL, Centro Astalli, and the Italian School System – all large in size, scope, and influence. Eventually, thousands of students connected to learn and explore the migration phenomenon and in turn strengthened the desire to have a global partnership for sustainable development. Coming full circle, student partnerships were the root of this project, reflecting the global youths desire to unite and work together, whether it be across an ocean or in a small community, in an effort to create a sustainable and equitable future for all.

For these partnerships to work effectively and create the desired impact (especially considering Next Chapters overseas collaboration), there had to be a constant exchange of information, with respect to the dynamics within each group involved. Language barrier was a challenge to be overcome, as we had two Italian speakers as part of the core team, which was vital to the success of the project. Active listening, patience, and empathy were key to our successes. Built into the nature of our experiences with social impact work, these factors were natural to us as a group when working with external partners. While working together as the core group of five, empathy and communication were crucial to the project's development; there were times where we had to ground ourselves and remind ourselves that we were working towards a common goal. We found there to be little support systems around us to facilitate the time required for growth of our projects, and so respectfully working together was integral to our successes.

For the Millennium Fellowship Class of 2021, UCL had a strong partnership with the Campus Directors (two students selected by MCN to lead their Campus Millennium Fellows), granting access to communication hubs and providing platforms to showcase project outcomes. To be able to benefit from this partnership, it was important to communicate effectively and have a strong structure in place while working with institutional protocols and schedules that are difficult to navigate. Much of the institute–student partnership was based on sharing project information on social media platforms and discussing how to engage students more in campus-based SDG initiatives and campaigns. I would like to see universities focus less on the public-facing side of social impact projects and look at how they can directly influence the growth of such projects within their systems and existing communities. It is crucial that institutions with the ability and means available do consider the barriers and challenges that their students may face when working on social impact projects; whether that be access to funding, technology, resources, or space. In an ideal world, universities would empower students within their institution and proactively remove hierarchy when collaborating. Social impact work is critical to improve our planet. Once universities truly recognize this, I believe student projects will truly thrive.

The Millennium Fellowship has been influential to my journey, on both a professional and personal level. As a Campus Director for 20 Fellows, it felt as though my leadership style was always under the spotlight. At times it was a challenge, but the Millennium Fellowship provided me with the tools and support systems to be an empathetic and confident leader. The connections I formed throughout my time in the Fellowship were both global and local, each encounter shaping who I am today. Originally unsure of which route I wanted to take after completion of my undergraduate degree, the Fellowship played a critical role in the decision to complete postgraduate education before taking a more hands-on role in social impact work, centred around meeting the SDGs. Overall, the Millennium Fellowship gave me hope. Overseeing, collaborating, and hearing about thousands of social impact projects globally was empowering, and truly sparked a fire that the global youth will prevail to create a liveable future. The innovation, determination, and desperation fuelling every student's project felt freeing and inspiring. MCN and the UNAI are changing the world and are inspiring hundreds of thousands of youth worldwide to do the same.

SHRIYA DAYAL

Millennium Fellow at Punjab Engineering College, India, Class of 2021

Creating the Conditions for Accountable Student–University Partnerships

During my bachelor's, I was the secretary of a student organization working on women's empowerment. Our work largely involved collaborations with other student groups. However, for many students, social impact was about holding placards and getting pictures taken. Hence, collaborations could often pose problems, demanding patience and diligence from the entire team.

As I begin to unpack the student dynamics at my university, I'd like to give you a glimpse into the kind of schooling these students were exposed to prior to receiving a university education. After spending their senior years at school preparing for competitive exams, most students who choose to embark on the journey towards admission into premier Indian institutes (in this case, engineering institutes) miss out on extracurricular activities and other aspects of social life. Naturally, when they enter university, they have little or no exposure to concepts like sustainability, let alone the 17 SDGs. Awareness of such concepts prior to university is highly dependent on the type of education received in schools and access to education beyond textbooks. While environmental conservation is a fairly common topic in the curricula, climate change, and sustainable development surface during extracurricular activities which are not mandatory. And so naturally, unless there is an interest in these subject areas, students delve into them only when they are required to.

By the time undergraduates reach their final year, they have already been moulded and redirected into new career pathways, primarily focusing on options that boost their self-esteem and grant a level of social stature in the eyes of family and friends. There are of course exceptions. With the increasing access to information and understanding of sustainability, many of them also choose to incorporate the SDGs into their careers. Universities, in this case, open up opportunities to deep dive once in a while and discover avenues in the sustainability field.

This is where youth leadership programs like the Millennium Fellowship save the day. Through the Millennium Fellowship, undergraduates like myself were exposed to not only training and guidance on social impact, but also a global community of like-minded people who aim to dedicate their lives to social issues. The fellowship helped us rediscover our communities and encourage other students around us to see their work through the lens of sustainability.

Over time, I realized that my university functioned like a system in itself. At the nuts-and-bolts level, it may seem like the students ran the whole system, but in reality, the power to operate lay in the hands of those higher in the administrative hierarchy.

During my fellowship, I used my role as the Secretary of the Women Empowerment Cell to lead my project on menstrual health awareness. We surveyed young people to understand their stance on menstrual health, the kind of taboos they were exposed to, and their personal beliefs. We realized our project that once focused on the rural communities outside our city should begin with the students on campus instead. This opened up many opportunities for collaboration and exchange of ideas.

While it is understandable for universities to allocate funding only for projects within the degree programs they offer, they have failed to assess the impact of externalities associated with their projects. Social impact projects are considered free-of-cost services, requiring one-day trips, and photographs for newsletters.

There are, commendably, many universities today that are not biased against social impact projects and offer support in the form of mentoring and funding. This is made possible by establishing a relationship of trust between the students and the university. Usually, a strong monitoring mechanism leads to lesser mishaps and propels the system towards efficiency. For example, a university sponsoring a student-led project may risk funds at the hands of dishonest team members. The risk can be avoided altogether with active monitoring of financial transactions and verification of billing details provided.

In addition to my Fellowship project, I had the opportunity to work on Climate Education in the state of Kerala (India) during my Fellowship. I worked with an NGO called Bring Back Green, which is pioneering climate education in schools and universities, and learnt about the social factors that enabled effective partnerships with universities and schools. Communities in Kerala are sensitive towards natural disasters and are actively working on disaster management and climate change mitigation. In addition, the Ministry of Education is supportive of incorporating the concept of sustainability into education and has approved the curriculum designed by Bring Back Green on the same. Bring Back Green was able to garner support and trust from the local citizens via numerous partnerships with schools and universities. These partnerships focused on upskilling teachers with knowledge of climate change and sensitizing students towards climate action. Direct engagement via capacity-building programs, workshops, and conferences has helped the organization garner support and trust from the local citizens and also acquire the necessary funds.

The receptivity of universities and schools to student-led collaboration facilitated by the NGO has fostered the growth of climate sensitivity and preventive actions taken by the local community. It is a testament to amazing things that can happen when universities support student-led initiatives with open hearts and a nurturing mindset.

SRIJAN BANIK

Millennium Fellow at Brac University, Bangladesh, Class of 2021

Co-creating With Community Partners

Being an impact entrepreneur is tough. There is no secret recipe for being successful – we have to jump through new obstacles every day. However, it gets tougher when we are students and trying to do this. No one teaches us how to take the first step in our social impact journey or how to keep solving all the new challenges every day. For the last two and a half years, I have been leading three different social impact projects. Throughout this journey, I have come across many different tools that helped me move forward. But the most powerful one was an effective partnership: a partnership between the communities, the stakeholders, my colleagues, my mentors, and my university.

During the pandemic, I created a decentralized education hub for the children in my community as all the schools shut down. As part of the project, I organized book exchange events where the students shared their favourite books and learned from each other by sharing their insights. I did not have a team there that could help me execute the project. A global pandemic kept me from even reaching out to my university friends. But the children in my community really wanted this to happen. I partnered with the children themselves to arrange the event. Some of them used their small network to connect us with more people, some of them volunteered with me to organize the logistics, and some gave me new ideas. So even though I did not have a team, the community itself became my team.

Although this is an example of community partnership on a very small scale, it helped me understand one crucial thing – *even the smallest of steps can turn into something impactful if we bring them together*. This project was a combination of small ideas and small steps that co-created an impact. All of us experience social issues and challenges in different ways, so when we partner up to think about a solution, different ways of thinking can create the most inclusive way to serve the community. That is what our universities should focus on, too. Having a platform to convene creative minds and change-makers to co-create an impact.

Being a student leader is hard, but there are many ways our universities can help. It can create collaborative hubs of impact leaders to mentor them and co-create solutions for creating positive change in society. It not only will equip the student changemakers to take on the challenges of being a social entrepreneur but will also create a strong network of social change. In the way my community partners helped me to connect with more people from their network, with proper collaboration, these small networks of student leaders in each university can connect with each other to expand to a global level to pioneer drastic positive changes! It all starts with a simple but effective partnership.

AYUSHI NAHAR

Millennium Fellow at O.P. Jindal Global University, India, Class of 2021

'The first partnership that any individual has is with themselves'

Walking through the gates of my pre-school after 15 years took me down a bittersweet road of nostalgia. Somewhere amidst the crowd of innocent and curious five-year olds, I spotted my five-year old self-walking confidently through the gates ready to conquer the day. Her radiating smile warmed the hearts of her friends and teachers, and her innocence provided her with an untainted lens to view the world of infinite possibilities. It is during this walk down memory lane that I realized that the first partnership that any individual has is with themselves. The sustainability of this partnership will determine all subsequent partnerships. While pursuing my Millennium Fellowship Project, The Financial Literacy Times, a project that aimed to raise financial awareness among women and children within my Jain community, as well as working with my father who donated and set up a Robotics and Artificial Intelligence Lab at the Indian Institute of Science, this facet of partnerships became clear to me. The relationship I shared with that five-year old laid down the foundation of my robust partnerships with my community, stakeholders, and institutions such as IISc.

A robust partnership is a two-way road, which, in my experience, is paved with humility, transparency, and the keenness to do the work. My first partnership for The Financial Literacy project was with my dad, who has his own company and has been in the investment sector for nearly three decades. This partnership thrived on my ability to listen, learn, and question, and his ability to break down the concept of investments, listen without judgement, and most importantly, encourage my endeavours. This strong educational, as well as biological, partnership translated to my partnerships with women in my community who weren't empowered or educated. This partnership was a slightly tricky one because it involved gaining their trust and respecting their cultural and traditional stance on their perception of financial independence/dependence, while simultaneously nudging them in the direction of economic empowerment. Some women believed that their husbands made financial decisions that were right for them and that there was no need to attain financial independence. While I didn't completely agree with that line of thought, it made me realize the importance of multiplicity of perspectives, or *anekanthvaadta*. These partnerships achieved the objective of reaching out to the primary stakeholder (i.e. women) with the solid support of my father (i.e. my mentor). My partnership with MCN also helped me immensely, as they have given me several opportunities to speak to leaders in the investment sector such as Mr Matt Patsky – CEO of Trillium Asset Management Company, USA and speak on panels which brought together the voices of university students working towards furthering the SDGs. Working and partnering with MCN shed light on the fact that a partnership with a student can be built with two key ingredients – the persistence of the student and the relentless support of an organization.

While the above project looks at a student–community partnership, the donation of the lab at IISc sheds light on a student–donor–university partnership. My brother and I felt that the institute would benefit from a robotics lab to bring to fruition ideas of students. Subsequently, my father donated and designed this lab without having the legal obligation to fulfil any corporate social responsibility (CSR) requirements. He actively involved us in this initiative and made us accompany him to meetings with the senior management of the institute to make the official donation, to witness handing over the key of the lab to us by IISc, and other aspects of this ambitious initiative. His partnership with IISc was based on his vision to redefine the standards of educational facilities in India, and he taught us the importance of doing a job with complete honesty.

This partnership brought about tangible changes and impacts at the university as well as national level. It taught me that if a university wants to make effective partnerships with students or potential investors they must primarily have a long-term vision. This vision must be complemented by a cultural ethos where innovation is supported by providing financing to students for meritorious projects, ensuring that funds of the university are invested in appropriate investment options, such as mutual funds to ensure the growth and liquidity of money (efficient financial management), and creating a cultural ethos of innovation among the students. The value of the college degree must not merely be associated with seeking a well-paying job. The purpose of a degree is to explore yourself, not box yourself in the job market. Lastly, universities must bridge the gap between the academia and the industry by building strong partnerships with MNCs, NGOs, investors (both CSR and non-CSR), companies, or organizations where students from their university can pursue internships and get work exposure.

A partnership – big or small – can have ripple effects that in turn have the potential to make waves in this ocean called the world. Partnerships and networking bring like-minded people together and enable the exchange of ideas and solutions. We live in a global village, and partnerships in this village have never been more integral than they are now. Consequently, the furtherance of SDG17 is the need of the hour, to say the least. Competition makes us faster, but collaboration makes us better.

HOW TO POWER STUDENT LEADERSHIP FOR THE SDGs: CONCRETE RECOMMENDATIONS

The insights and reflections above make clear that student leaders are essential collaborators to advance the SDGs. Based on nearly a decade implementing the Millennium Fellowship, I want to share concrete recommendations to power your own civic initiatives on campuses worldwide:

1. Trust Students

In recent years many leading voices have advocated for community-driven development. The idea is to move away from prescriptive approaches and instead engage community leaders in decision-making. A good example is Partners in Health, a grassroots network with 98% of its nearly 20,000 strong workforce based in local communities in 11 nations.

The Millennium Fellowship has followed the same logic in engaging with students. We trust students' power, ideas, and voices. Rather than telling students what community issues to address, we invite Fellowship applicants to propose initiatives based on proximate local challenges they view as priorities. Students can tell when they are being authentically valued and validated. By using the SDGs as an organizing framework and including a relatively big tent of what Fellowship applicants can potentially qualify for, the program has grown exponentially. My best advice: regularly convene student leaders committed to making a difference, ask them how the institution can be most supportive of their work, keep pre-existing assumptions out, and co-create with students and community partners.

2. Challenge Students

Our core curriculum has been refined over the years. Its origins stem from my colleague Abigail's service in the Peace Corps and review of 30 leadership curricula. One of the core lessons Abigail shared is that we need to help move students away from what she termed 'heropreneurship'. Students should question why they are engaged in social impact initiatives and how they can show up as effective sidekicks with community partners.

We recognize that advancing social impact can be difficult, and we want young leaders to feel affirmed in recognizing and leveraging their power to make a difference. At the same time, Abigail often defended that we should not end up propping up systems that perpetuate inequities in the process. To put it simply: we need young leaders who can critically assess their own contributions and the real impact they are having in communities. Young leaders can cause harm if ego and prioritization of their own self-interests minimize the important work and partnerships being cultivated. The goal is to help emerging leaders cultivate discernment as a practice.

3. Celebrate Students

Young leaders often learn in the classroom how to solve problems in a linear fashion. Creating social impact, with so many variables and inputs, can be highly complex and at times an uneven and lonely path. When students make tangible contributions in society, it is important to lift up those leaders and their experiences. In practice, we've seen this take several forms. University leaders have met with their cohorts of Millennium Fellows to learn directly from them on their Fellowship Projects. They have recorded video messages with their Fellows, published campus articles about Fellows' initiatives, and shared these across their communities.

We have also seen that one of the most powerful forms of celebration costs no money and transforms lives: mentorship. University faculty and staff have advised Millennium Fellows, working closely with them on a weekly basis. This investment of time, coupled with amplification of initiatives, are cost-effective, high impact pathways to accelerate student leadership for the SDGs.

4. Incentivize Collaboration for Impact

There are many barriers to effective partnerships on campuses. For example, students often split time between their studies, co-curricular commitments, family commitments, and part-time or full-time jobs. When students make a concrete commitment to giving back, universities are uniquely positioned to remove barriers to engagement and incentivize effective collaborations.

To remove barriers, universities can provide academic credit for students' civic leadership. Universities can also provide funding or stipends for students actively engaged in the community. Beyond this, to borrow an idea Millennium Fellow Srijan Banik of BRAC University shared above, a university can create a collaborative hub for students to learn from and partner with each other and with other stakeholders. There is so much potential here.

In many of the universities we visit, there are often multiple organizations and ventures advancing the SDGs on a single campus. The challenge: they often compete for the same resources: for the engagement of student volunteers, funding, and faculty and administrative support. A university can set up a physical space for students committed to the SDGs to meet periodically – either with an open agenda, one centred on sharing best practices, or to explore collaborating on larger, campus-wide initiatives. For example, one of the cornerstones of the Fellowship curriculum is peer to peer feedback. Fellows have lived experiences and learn from successes and failures. During Fellowship sessions throughout the semester, Fellows are invited to share a current challenge they are facing in their community initiative and receive feedback from their peers.

If funding is available to support students' participation in these meetings that can enable more students to engage. If not, then consider non-financial resources that can still help students carve out time to collaborate: certificates of recognition or an offer to help advise collaborative students with their partnerships or professional pursuits.

5. Model Ethical, Collaborative Leadership

The best way we can cultivate the visionary, transformative leadership of Gen Z is to model core values in our own daily practices. Dr Saleem Badat, former Vice-Chancellor of Rhodes University in South Africa and current Consulting Fellow to the Andrew W. Mellon Foundation, shares the following outlook:

> *[O]ur commitment to ethical leadership is not just a single course. Universities should be living themselves as ethical institutions. That's the best way to model behavior for your students .... From the top, from the Vice-Chancellor, throughout the institution, you should be modeling the idea of ethics and ethical leadership, rather than just doing it at the level of course work .... (UDC-TV)*

In 15 years in this space, we have seen university leaders and institutions that centre-students and their civic commitments. Universities that prioritize their relationships with community partners and ensure there are proactive channels and spaces for co-creation. This leadership dramatically accelerates progress for the SDGs.

Conversely, there are examples of university leaders losing jobs and causing harm by acting in ways completely incongruous with their mandates. I point to the insight of Millennium Fellow Ayushi Nahar of O.P. Jindal Global University in India. She shared above, 'I realized that the first partnership that any individual has is with themselves. The sustainability of this partnership will determine all subsequent partnerships'. We need university leaders at all levels who model the highest standards that we hope students will emulate and build upon.

In addition, we have seen examples of universities seeking to turn partnerships into stories of heroic students and faculty 'saving the world', while minimizing the core contributions made by communities they engage with. In other cases, universities take all the credit for community-led or student-initiated partnerships. In these cases, meaningful progress that can change lives is being overshadowed by narrow interests. This can lead to distrust and discontentment. It is important for institutions to exercise organizational humility, just as we call on students to do.

Finally, universities can model collaborative leadership. When we started sharing the Millennium Fellowship nine years ago, some universities were reluctant, claiming they already provided the best programming in the sector. Entrepreneurial institutions recognized that external opportunities and networks do not compete with their own programs; they complement and bolster them. Nine years later, some of those campuses that were on the sidelines are now actively promoting the program and touting their Fellows' leadership. It is imperative that universities provide their students with the infrastructure to make a difference: a multilane highway of opportunities to public service rather than a single road. Engage networks like the UNAI and the University Global Coalition to learn about and leverage opportunities like the Millennium Fellowship to complement what is already underway on campus.

By trusting, challenging, and celebrating students, by incentivizing collaboration, and by modelling ethical, collaborative leadership, universities can have an exponentially larger impact in advancing the SDGs. In the process, they will cultivate a new generation of leaders that make the SDGs core to their purpose and lives. Leaders who, when they were at university, learned how to effectively partner with others for a larger goal. Training effective collaborators for the SDGs would be among the most powerful contributions of universities in this decade. This can be manifested by each person reading this book and by the partners you engage. Summer Wyatt shared that her Millennium Fellowship experience 'sparked a fire that the global youth will prevail to create a livable future'. It is our collective responsibility to help young leaders to protect and grow that passion and conviction for a more just world.

REFERENCE

UDC-TV. *Higher education today: Dr. Saleem Badat, Vice-Chancellor, Rhodes University* [Video]. YouTube. https://youtu.be/plC0ZfYeoaQ

7

GLOBAL SHARED LEARNING BY TECNOLÓGICO DE MONTERREY: AN INTERNATIONAL PARTNERSHIP FOR SUSTAINABLE DEVELOPMENT EDUCATION

Luz Patricia Montaño-Salinas and
José Manuel Páez-Borrallo

ABSTRACT

The COVID-19 pandemic accelerated the digital transformation at universities and forced a rapid transition to online education. Tecnológico de Monterrey leveraged its experience in online education to develop and scale a program of collaborative courses with international partners on the United Nation Sustainable Development Goals (UN SDGs). The pilot program, based on Collaborative Online International Learning (COIL), and focused on the UN SDGs, aimed to provide international experiences to students who were not able to study abroad due to economic reasons (SUNY Collaborative Online International Learning). The formula involves two professors who co-design and co-teach an online subject or part of the syllabus to their joint cohort of students, highlighting the relevant elements associated with those subjects' contents included in the UN SDGs. However, generating enough courses that reached a considerable number of students and involved an international diversity of partners and topics, added layers of difficulty. For instance, not all academics were prepared to manage an online joint group of students or to introduce concepts of the UN SDGs in their courses. To solve these problems and scale up these courses, we created 'Global Shared Learning – Classroom' a program that addresses the necessary elements of faculty matching, joint planning of subjects, online co-teaching, use of technological tools, and the active participation of students. Today we have involved more than 18,000 students and 500 professors from 150 universities. This chapter shows how capacity building and complementary partnerships were built. It includes the elements to design, replicate the model, and overcome technology issues for other universities asking to be part of this program.

Keywords: Education; United Nation Sustainable Development Goal; Collaborative Online International Learning; internationalization; co-teaching; technology

UN SDG17: SCOPE AND DIVERSITY

Focusing on education, Irina Bokova, Director-General of UNESCO argued that

> *fundamental change is needed in the way we think about education's role in global development because it has a catalytic impact on the well-being of individuals and the future of our planet. Now, more than ever, education has a responsibility to be in gear with 21st-century challenges and aspirations and foster the right types of values and skills that will lead to sustainable and inclusive growth, and peaceful living together.* (UNESCO, 2017)

Global collaboration among higher education institutions (HEIs) doubtlessly can help achieve four of the SDG17 targets. The potential of 250 million tertiary students today, plus the research and educational capabilities of 7 million researchers and professors can speed up the objectives in at least the following SDG17 targets: 17.6 'Knowledge sharing and cooperation for access to science, technology and innovation'; 17.8 'Strengthen the science, technology and innovation capacity for least-developed countries'; 17.9 'Enhanced SDG capacity in developing countries'; and 17.16 'Enhance the global partnership for sustainable development' (United Nations, *Goal 17*).

Academic collaboration among HEIs is an established practice where university networks, associations, or interest groups join forces to develop activities of all kinds, aligning programs and exploiting synergies, that seek to improve their performance and impact. Collaboration is the essence of SDG17 and, in recent times, many university networks have committed to addressing the SDGs by leveraging their academic, research, and outreach capabilities, more specifically for 17.6 and 17.16 targets. Raising awareness and bringing out the relevance of certain SDGs among students and teachers in their daily educational materials or research projects have become fundamental elements in the missions of many HEIs.

HEI NETWORKS AND ASSOCIATIONS WITH SDG PROGRAMS

Some existing HEI consortia or networks have created clusters or groups of interest focused on the SDGs in their work agendas or were created specifically to address the SDGs in HEI. Here we highlight a few:

1. Universitas 21, a global network of 28 universities whose Steering Committee made a declaration to specifically support SDG4 and SDG17. To this end, it has internally launched some programs, like the 'Real Impact on Society and Environment' (RISE), supporting student-led projects (Universitas 21, *U21's Commitment*).
2. The Association of Pacific Rim Universities (APRU), a regional network of 60 universities in the Pacific Rim region seeks to develop specific collaborative programs in key areas of focus such as 'Shaping Higher Education in the Asia Pacific', 'Creating Global Student Leaders', 'Asia-Pacific Challenges', and a 'Sustainable Waste Management Program' (APRU, *Our Work*).

3. The Hemispheric Universities Consortium (HUC), a group of 14 universities across Latin America, the Caribbean, Canada, and the USA, aims to collaborate and facilitate problem-based collaborations in education, research, and innovation aligning and acting upon the UN SDGs with joint programs such as 'Hemispheric Student Dialogues on the SDGs' (Hemispheric University Consortium, *Who We Are)*.
4. University Global Coalition, a global consortium of 150+ universities, HEIs networks, and SDG-related associations created to engage higher education leaders in integrating SDG strategy throughout teaching, research, and operations, and helping to facilitate collaboration among institutions (University Global Coalition, *About*).
5. The Sustainable Development Solutions Network specifically recognizes the SDGs in academic activities and as a strong commitment for individual HEIs.

THE SDGs AT TECNOLÓGICO DE MONTERREY: STRATEGY AND PROGRAMS

Tecnológico de Monterrey has developed its 2025 Sustainability and Climate Change Plan, including objectives and actions to face the global climate emergency (Tecnológico de Monterrey, 2021).

THE SIX STRATEGIC AREAS

The six strategic areas that the institution will work on as part of its plan for 2025: Culture of Sustainability, Mitigation, Adaptation, Education, Research, and Outreach.

Having established the strategic areas that the institution would focus on, we decided that the Global Shared Learning (GSL) – Classroom could add to the achievement of our institutional objectives if we directed the work of each of the collaborations towards two of them: education and outreach, as through the activities developed in teaching collaborations, a better understanding of the SDGs could be promoted to students and teachers.

Applying the UN SDG principles as a framework for peer collaborations proved to be highly successful, as it also provided a common basis for dialogue to design activities from a shared point of interest. The conversations and negotiations were faster and more efficient since from the beginning both academics had a common goal.

For students, it has also represented an interesting exercise in which they create a greater awareness of the importance of working towards the achievement of the UN SDG objectives by having the opportunity to link their reality with the reality described by their peers globally. This experience would be more difficult to achieve if it only depended on a model based on physical mobility, so the model based on technological tools and distance education is very suitable, accessible, and easily scalable to reach the largest number of students and teachers in participating institutions, thus accelerating the path towards the goal.

An additional element is that more and more academics conceive of interdisciplinary collaborations as an experience offering opportunities to understand and solving significant problems to improve the human condition. This aspect of collaborations is still incipient, but we see great potential in it.

STRATEGIC PROGRAMS

In order to engage the academic community and drive progress in achieving the goals established in the 2030 Strategic Plan (Tecnológico de Monterrey, 2019), the programs generated in the different areas of the institution are structured in such a way that a shared information platform serves as the basis for larger and more ambitious projects and programs:

a) Lifelong Learning Green Academy, a project to train private sector leaders in sustainability and climate change.
b) Credit-bearing courses that include the SDGs. Every semester, Tecnológico de Monterrey invites its professors to be trained in the teaching of the SDGs and to address in their courses the analysis and understanding of some of them. By design some of the courses that grant academic credit include SDG-related

topics, understanding, and actions towards the fulfilment of the goals established in the SDGs.

c) Educational Resources – Tecnológico de Monterrey. The academic community of Tecnológico de Monterrey provides a series of resources to the general public and other teachers that can serve to improve understanding of the challenges and goals established in the SDGs.

SDGs IN EDUCATION AT TECNOLÓGICO DE MONTERREY: THE GSL INITIATIVE

Although international student mobility was already very relevant at Tecnológico de Monterrey in 2018, the team from the Vice Rectory for International Affairs raised the question of how to increase international experience for our students, especially for students with financial or personal barriers to participating in-person in an international program.

Taking into account the years of experience in online education and the propensity of our faculty to innovate, we decided to bring the international experience home through the COIL model. Our prior experiences with COIL had a relatively low success rate, so we modified the original COIL model by introducing the role of the 'Global Classroom Coordinator' (Fig. 7.1).

The 'Global Classroom Coordinator' is in charge of ensuring the path of collaboration and adherence to the COIL model and advises participating faculty on pedagogical and technology issues. They also support the back-office functions that come with academic administration. The role of the 'Global Classroom Coordinator' is present in all stages, from co-design to delivery, and it has proven to be an instrumental element to guarantee a higher success rate and a satisfactory experience for both faculty and students.

Our first pilot with the modified COIL model was in August 2018 and provided a satisfactory number of international collaborations. However, to have a bigger impact on the daily life of our institution and to offer more international choices to our students, we needed to increase the number of collaborations. That led us to run a new pilot in February 2019 with a greater number of

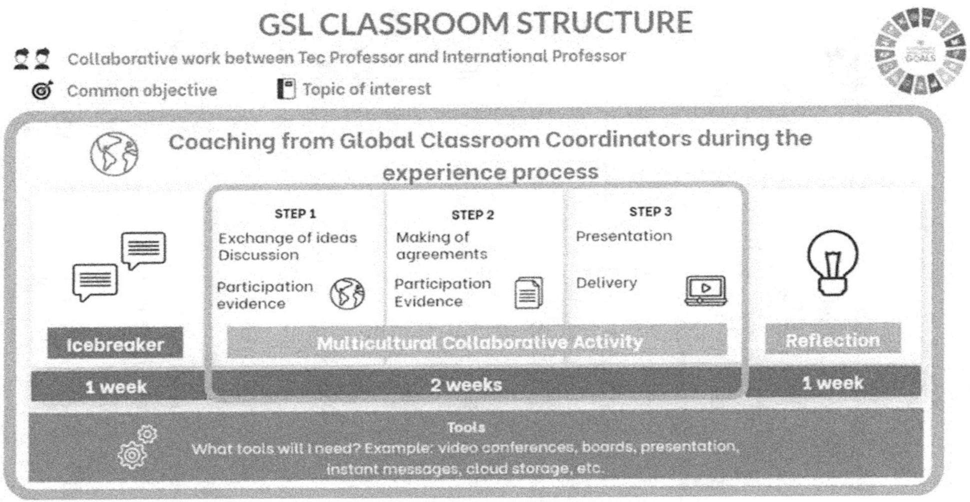

Fig. 7.1. Modified COIL Model for its Implementation at the Tecnológico de Monterrey.

collaborations, which gave us invaluable insights into the process, inputs, and complexity of establishing a common foundation for collaborative work. The topics proposed by teachers were highly diverse since there was no common thread to guide the interest of the participants. This diversity of subject matter resulted in extra time needed for analysis and discussion to reach agreements on the class topics.

How could we generate a common platform of interest for courses from so many diverse disciplines?

The concept of the SDGs as a fundamental element in higher education was gaining currency at Tecnológico de Monterrey, as in many other universities. The inclusion of sustainability issues in the curriculum was seen as a central educational component for new generations and its relevance for research was gaining supporters in our institution at all levels. We discovered a great opportunity to open and expand knowledge of the SDGs at the core of the educational process with the collaboration of our international partners, which helped to improve the collective awareness of our teaching and student bodies in a cultural and global environment different from their own.

As in many other organizations, changes and new projects do not happen in isolation. Just as Tecnológico de Monterrey was moving forward with its Sustainability & Climate Change Plan, the new educational model TEC21 was launched in August 2019 (Issuu, Tecnológico de Monterrey, 2020). TEC21 incorporates educational elements different from the typical master class, and thus encouraged us to amplify the scope of the GSL-Classroom and think of ways to incorporate new elements into Global Classroom model. These factors led us to establish the SDGs as the basis for collaboration between international peers in a Global Classroom. The new expertise in our modified COIL model, the use of technological tools, and a common learning objective based on the academic relevancy of the SDGs were the perfect combination for the TEC21 model as an activity that adds value and facilitates internationalization at home.

In August 2019, we ran the first cohort of collaborations with this new SDG analysis requirement integrated into the course discipline. The formal introduction of SDGs was highly successful, as it provided a common goal among academics. Furthermore, it provided a framework on which to focus their design approaches and efforts to help students learn about the SDGs.

GSL-CLASSROOM AND SDG CAPACITY BUILDING

The original COIL model is quite intuitive and can easily be adopted with minimal training. There are many online courses and extensive and detailed information shared on specialized sites about COIL (SUNY Collaborative Online International Learning, *COIL Resources*). In order to guarantee a common base of understanding and knowledge of our model at Tecnológico de Monterrey, we designed a capacity building program that helps faculty learn about COIL and our adaptation. As part of the training program, faculty develop a course proposal they can use to apply to the call for courses in the upcoming semester campaign of Global Classroom courses.

In this training module on the Global Classroom model, teachers learn about the different components that make up COIL and how to get the most out of each of them: design steps, technological tools, digital platforms, and apps to enrich the student's experience, as well as concepts to create a digital environment to strengthen the links between participants, deepen the analysis and discussion of the topics, and facilitate the approach to culturally sensitive issues.

After having managed the 2018 and 2019 pilots, we realized the way SDGs were taught was very uneven. Some professors delved too deeply into details, which made the collaboration more complex than necessary. Others intended to cover too many SDGs, and some had a very superficial approach.

The administration and support team of GSL-Classroom are not SDG specialists, so taking action to standardize the treatment of the SDGs was not straightforward. Tecnológico de Monterrey had assigned the management strategy for commitments to the SDGs in the Vice Presidency of Inclusion, Social Impact, and Sustainability (VPISIS). A cooperation agreement between this office and the International Vice Rectory set up guidelines for faculty to manage the SDGs appropriately to have a real impact on their development as an institution.

As part of the improvements suggested by VPISIS, we included a training module on 'Education for Sustainable Development' (ESD), providing teachers with tools to design collaborative activities and to better understand ESD teaching techniques. This ESD training module is a collaboration between internal units at Tecnológico de Monterrey and other invited partners.

This model highlights the importance of partnerships between universities, not only for mobility and research, but also for joint teaching and training of new generations of academics who can further incorporate study, analysis, and reflection on the SDGs in future leadership roles.

The training processes of the GSL-Classroom model plus the ESD model have produced very interesting, well-structured, and academically robust collaboration proposals that add value to the course syllabus. Currently, this training program is offered only to Tecnológico de Monterrey professors. We are reviewing the possibility of opening this same process to professors from participating partner universities in the future.

We trust that through this training track we will consolidate a critical mass of faculty who will lead advancement in the teaching of the SDGs and their inclusion in all subjects, with or without the addition of GSL-Classroom.

COVID-19 AND THE GSL PROGRAM AT TECNOLÓGICO DE MONTERREY

As previously detailed, the Global Classroom program began due to the need to offer some form of internationalization at home for students who, for various reasons, could not participate in an international experience that involved relocation.

The pilots carried out in 2018 and 2019 indicated that we had a model that could help us achieve the goal of internationalization at home, thus expanding our catalogue of internationalization opportunities. By the end of the Fall 2019 semester, we had 12 courses, including a Global Classroom collaboration ready to be delivered in Spring 2020. We closed 2019 with the conviction that 2020 would be a year of growth and expansion of collaborations.

The start of the Spring 2020 semester was like any other; little did we imagine that less than five weeks after the semester began, our presidency would make the historic decision to cease activities for two weeks to prepare for the transfer of all face-to-face courses (more than 32,000) to digital format due to the imminent presence of the COVID-19 virus and its impact on Mexican society.

The impact of COVID-19 on the plans for internationalization of our students was direct and forceful. All partners began to communicate actions they would take to protect their communities. Among them were recalling students studying abroad back to their home campus and sending non-native students studying on their campuses home to their countries of origin. Tecnológico de Monterrey was no exception, and as of 23 March 2021, we began the process of repatriating students and educating virtually.

If internationalization is only conceived through physical mobility, we had a scenario in which this activity was completely annulled, with no possible date to re-establish itself. Governments took tough positions regarding migration and transit between borders, reaching the point of completely 'shielding' the country and eliminating mobility of any kind.

How then could we offer our students the option of an international experience? How could we offer a space for conversation that would allow understanding between societies in a situation as serious as a pandemic? Joint collaborations and the use of all online tools were the most practical response, and the Global Classroom model we had been implementing was the best way to keep our students and teachers connected to the world.

SCALING THE GSL-CLASSROOM

Despite the restrictions that COVID-19 imposed on the operation of universities, we were able to carry out the commitments we made to collaborate with partners. The collaboration generated spectacular results because our students and our partners were eager to communicate, collaborate, get to know each other, and express their empathy towards each other.

This success did not go unnoticed by our academic authorities, who immediately requested the scaling of the model to cover at least 100 courses per semester for the next 2.5 years. Regardless of the course that the pandemic took in Mexico and in the world, the students and faculty of Tecnológico de Monterrey would have permanent access to these types of activities.

Until the Spring 2020 semester, scaling of this program had been very controlled, as our capacity was small. With the support expressed by our Rector, we obtained sufficient resources to expand our capacity, and, by December 2022, partner with more than 513 groups in collaborations with 255 partner universities (Fig. 7.2).

Our activity gave rise to collaboration with more than 30 partner universities, some who were our long-time collaborators, others with whom we established a joint project for the first time. The latter has been particularly enriching for us because it has allowed us to generate collaboration spaces that would not have been possible to discover through a traditional approach. Our partner universities are situated in Argentina, Australia, Belgium, Bolivia, Brazil, Canada, Chile, China, Colombia, Croatia, Cuba, Dominican Republic, Ecuador, Germany, India, Indonesia, Italy, Japan, the Netherlands, Panama, Peru, Philippines, Puerto Rico, Romania, Spain, South Korea, Taiwan, the UK, the USA, and Venezuela.

The increase in GSL-Classroom offerings also gave rise to an increase in the variety of subjects, which resulted in more schools internally engaging their teachers (Fig. 7.3).

As in any period of growth, logistics problems and administrative work were magnified; however, the collaborative spirit and enthusiasm of our students and faculty have helped reduce this burden and ensured an experience that both academics and students have found extraordinary.

Although the pandemic has lessened its disastrous effects on many regions of the world, we continue offering courses with the Global Classroom component. Conceived to open new

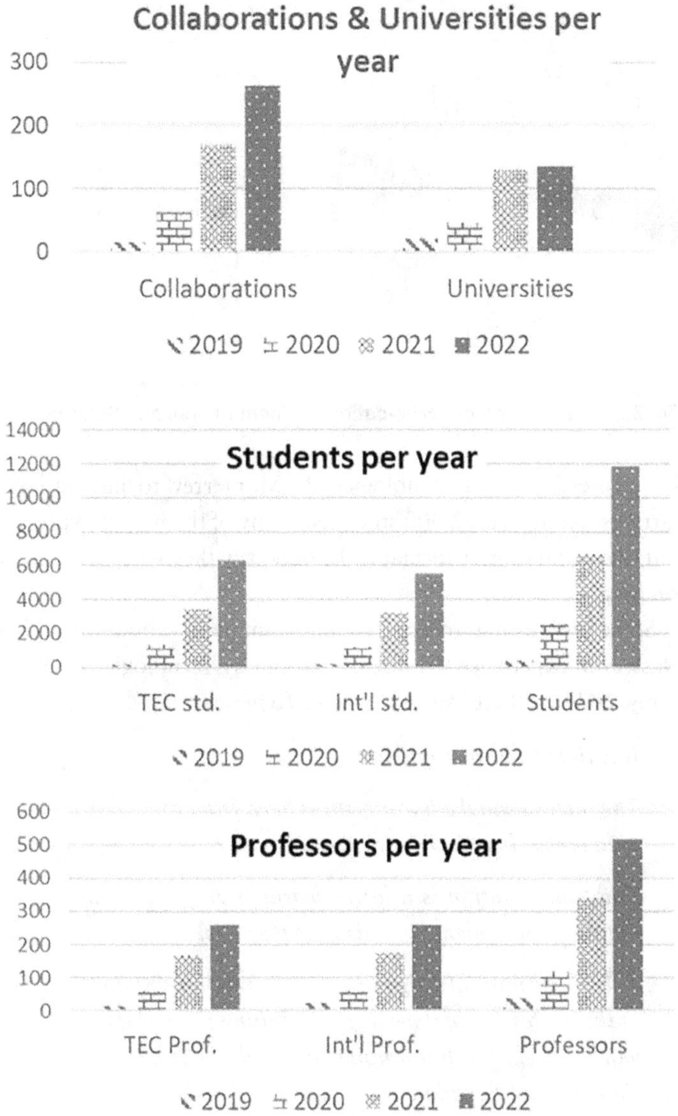

Fig. 7.2. Number of Collaborations, Universities, Students and Professors Involved in the GSL-Classroom From August 2018 to June 2022.

international opportunities to students, the results have exceeded our expectations by establishing new faculty connections and links. From January to December 2022, we have connected more than

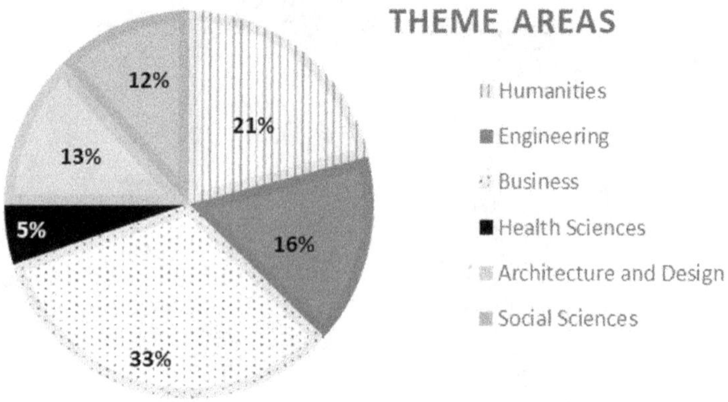

Fig. 7.3. Distribution of Participation by Theme Areas and Schools.

500 professors from Tecnológico de Monterrey to international partners and served 12,000 students. Many of them have expressed that this collaborative format is the only way they wish to continue teaching.

Some interesting reflections and comments about the GSL-Classroom experience (Global Classroom by Tecnológico de Monterrey, 2021a, 2021b, and *SUNY-Tec Experience*):

> *It is time to be disruptive.*
>
> *The international environment is lived from the classroom even when there is no such a classroom.*
>
> *This collaboration is a lot of learning and development, not only for students but also for teachers.*
>
> *There was not only a great working relationship with all of the professors in the courses ... I think there was a good working relationship among the students from Mexico, Canada, and Ecuador.*
>
> *You have to make your own informed opinion, which helps you to become a better student and to become a better citizen in today's world.*
>
> *What I enjoyed the most was the theme of the GSL-Week, diversity in general, but also the focus on gender, human rights, and worldviews.*

> *Many of my students came to the class with the perception that the Mexican people will be like the people we see in the news ... and that these people should be feared and somehow they are less than Americans, but through the COIL experience, my students, working with Jesus' students ... their whole dynamic was flipped, and they realized that your students are better educated, they're more dedicated, they're more mature ... so their whole perspective was changed ... I think it's a very good accomplishment to break down stereotypes ....*

GSL INITIATIVE: THE STAGES OF BUILDING A PROGRAM

As time passed without the possibility of physical mobility opening up, the pressure for a greater number of virtual opportunities for internationalization began to grow. The university initiated the change of the teaching–learning model in Autumn 2019, and the new model presented interesting opportunities to introduce ad hoc international activities such as Tec Week. These activities had initially been conceived face-to-face but, given the conditions, they would have to change. The continuation of the pandemic and the generation of this new model with new demands for internationalization led us to look for a format that could serve to link 'Tec Weeks' with groups of international teachers and students with similar interests. Reviewing the Global Classroom model, we built a spin-off that included the focus on the SDGs, the structure of collaboration, a support team, and the link with strategic partners of Tecnológico de Monterrey.

The new format was called 'Global Shared Learning – Week' (GSL-Week). GSL-Week brought challenges to joint design, as a week is a very short time for collaboration, and the dates of the weeks had been preset by administration. 'Tec Weeks' are anchored in weeks 6th and 12th of any academic semester.

An unexpected but very positive result we found with our proposal was the great interest of our partners in participating with Tecnológico de Monterrey in a Global Classroom course. However, some were a bit intimidated by the length, the demand for co-design, and even the use of specific technology, as they did not have much experience in some of these areas. To alleviate this indecision, we offered the option to participate in a 'GSL-Week' collaboration as a preliminary step. This was very attractive for many partners, as it allowed them to prepare for a greater commitment to a Global Classroom. Our 'GSL-Week' has now become a hotbed of potential partners for Global Classroom.

In the same way that Tecnológico de Monterrey actively sought internationalization options at home, other universities and organizations did as well. Tecnológico's participation in consortiums that include a large group of universities with similar profiles allowed us to identify another type of internationalization opportunity that we tested and was attractive for our students: micro-credentials. Short courses that award a badge and support a set of specific knowledge with or without curricular value have emerged with two constituencies: universities and companies searching for continuous training focused on professional updating or 'Lifelong Learning'.

At Tecnológico de Monterrey, we have selected courses based on the following criteria:

a) Maintain the focus on the SDGs.
b) Online delivery.
c) Ensure synchronous and asynchronous interaction of the participants.
d) Offer a cosmopolitan and multidisciplinary environment.
e) Have a length no longer than four weeks to match with the Tec21 educational model.

Fortunately, we found this structure in various consortiums to which we belong, such as APRU, U21, HUC, and European Consortium of Innovative Universities. In the same way that this initiative did not go unnoticed by our authorities, the performance of these activities during the pandemic was noted by the consortiums in which we participate. In May 2022, Universitas 21 gave us an award for the innovation that our GSL-Classroom model presented as an outstanding contribution to the internationalization of higher education (Universitas 21, 2022).

The response and acceptance by academics and students have been phenomenal, which encourages us to continue pursuing this format even when we return to face-to-face learning.

The urgency to correct deficiencies generated by the pandemic was overwhelming, but we managed to create a space to reflect and analyse everything we had built to keep our students and teachers connected to the world and develop the skills and competencies they will require for their futures.

By the end of Summer 2020, we had 'GSL-Classroom' that offered an international component for semester courses, 'GSL-Week' offered a one-off collaboration in weeks 6 and 12 of each semester, 'Global-Micro-credentials' offered various online activities on current issues, and the permanent offer of the Tecnológico de Monterrey of semester courses that had enrolled international students for more than 30 years. These four models composed a body of study that only lacked a name and the formal declaration of its structure. This is how we established the 'Global Shared Learning Initiative', an official framework that gives coherence to the indicated programs and that establishes the essential characteristics for the design of new programs that contribute to internationalization at Tecnológico de Monterrey.

The basic characteristics of any program in the GSL Initiative are:

- Designed or adapted to focus on teaching and reflecting on the SDGs.
- Uses technological tools for online work.
- Offers synchronous and asynchronous sessions for cross-team collaboration.
- Guarantees a multicultural environment in which Mexican and foreign students will work together.
- Offers, as far as possible, a multidisciplinary and collaborative environment where students from different areas of knowledge interact.

To ensure cohesion, we also gave them a common name and their own graphic identity. Today, depending on the format and duration, we call the collaborative online experiences: GSL-Classroom, GSL-Week, GSL-Micro-credentials), and the virtual exchange of semester subjects (GSL-Exchange). At Tecnológico de Monterrey, we envision the GSL initiative as the melting pot in which we can continue adding new programs that enrich internationalization at home.

The complete offer that emerges from the GSL initiative complements the already vast offering of in-person mobility in its different formats. Tecnológico de Monterrey's students have a rich range of opportunities, especially for those who participate and wish to develop skills and competencies that will make them stand out in the international job market, making them better professionals and citizens of the world, aware of the role they play in the future of society and humanity as a whole.

LESSONS LEARNED

As with many efforts of this magnitude, most see only the final result; however, we cannot close this narrative without acknowledging that the current results have been possible thanks to four components that Tecnológico de Monterrey worked on long before the pandemic, long before the SDGs were declared, and which many universities could utilize to improve their results:

- The development and care of significant relationships between peers that become strategic relationships based on trust and the interest in common growth.
- Investing in technology for teaching and learning. The experience that Tecnológico de Monterrey has in online education is the result of addressing this need to reach all corners of our country and bring higher education closer to more people. We have shown that distance education with the right educational technology and the right pedagogical model is just as valuable as in-person education.
- The commitment to progress in the SDGs as an institutional priority, designating physical and human resources to guide the institution towards specific institutional goals in which all areas (academics, staff, counsellors, alumni, and parents) are involved and actively participate.

- A specialized and committed team to support and accompany students and professors through the whole experience.

These results and advancements have been possible thanks to a dedicated team of talented people here with us at the Innovation for Internationalization and Networks Direction at the Vice Rectory for International Affairs, without whom this journey would have been impossible.

We cannot close this narrative without asking ourselves: what next? We do not have total clarity about the future. The pandemic is not over yet. However, we are confident we are on the right track, and with the company and collaboration of all our strategic partners, we will reach a worthwhile destination.

REFERENCES

Association of Pacific Rim Universities (APRU). *Our work*. https://apru.org/our-work/pacific-rim-challenges/unsdg/

Global Classroom by Tecnológico de Monterrey. (2021a). *Global week: Diversity in a globalized work*. [YouTube]. Retrieved November 8, 2022 from https://www.youtube.com/watch?v=48TX0fChh20

Global Classroom by Tecnológico de Monterrey. (2021b). Testimonials of students and professors. [YouTube]. Retrieved November 8, 2022 from https://www.youtube.com/watch?v=2d_yWZVhdAw&t=71s

Global Classroom by Tecnológico de Monterrey. (2022, November 8), SUNY-Tec experience. (not published).

Hemispheric University Consortium. Who we are. Retrieved November 8, 2022, from https://www.thehuc.org/

Issuu, Tecnológico de Monterrey. (2020). *Folleto Profesional*. Retrieved November 8, 2022, from https://issuu.com/tecdemty/docs/folleto_profesional_2020_ingles_05.09.20

SUNY Collaborative Online International Learning. COIL resources at SUNY. https://online.suny.edu/introtocoil/coil-resources-suny/

SUNY Collaborative Online International Learning. *Intro 2 COIL*. Retrieved November 8, 2022, from https://online.suny.edu/introtocoil/

Tecnológico de Monterrey. (2019, May). Towards 2030. https://internationalfaculty.tec.mx/sites/g/files/vgjovo821/files/2030-Strategic-Plan%20Tec%20de%20Monterrey.pdf

Tecnológico de Monterrey. (2021). *Strategic plan 2025 Tecnológico de Monterrey*. https://tec.mx/en/strategicplan2025#

UNESCO. (2017). Education for sustainable development goals: Learning objectives. https://unesdoc.unesco.org/ark:/48223/pf0000247444

United Nations. Goal 17. Department of Economic and Social Affairs. Retrieved November 8, 2022, from https://sdgs.un.org/goals/goal17

Universitas 21. (2022). *U21 award winners 2022*. Retrieved November 8, 2022, from https://universitas21.com/get-involved/u21-awards/u21-awards/u21-award-winners-2022

Universitas 21. *U21's commitment to the sustainable development goals*. Retrieved November 8, 2022 from https://universitas21.com/what-we-do/u21s-commitment-sdgs

University Global Coalition. *About*. Retrieved November 8, 2022, from https://universityglobalcoalition.org/about/

8

DRAWDOWN GEORGIA BUSINESS COMPACT: A PARTNERSHIP ADVANCING COLLECTIVE ACTION FOR CLIMATE MITIGATION

Marilyn A. Brown, Jasmine Crowe, John Lanier, Michael Oxman, Roy Richards and L. Beril Toktay

ABSTRACT

Now more than ever, climate action requires both private and public investment in building a sustainable future for all. COP26 affirmed the importance of collective action at all scales coupled with supporting public policy to limit global warming to a 1.5-degree trajectory. This chapter outlines the process and building blocks that culminated in the launch of the Drawdown Georgia Business Compact, whose mission is to leverage the collective impact of Georgia's business community to achieve net zero carbon emissions in the state by 2050. In bringing together companies across diverse industries, the Business Compact creates a community of practice where cross-sector collaboration accelerates Georgia's path to actualizing COP26's decarbonization vision while also considering 'beyond carbon' issues such as the economy, equity, public health, and the environment. This is a regional and voluntary approach to Sustainable Development Goal (SDG) 17 (Strengthen the means of implementation and revitalize the Global Partnership for Sustainable Development), which recognizes multi-stakeholder partnerships as important vehicles to achieve SDGs.

Keywords: SDG 17; climate action; voluntary business coalition; carbon reduction roadmapping; equity; drawdown

1. CREATING THE DRAWDOWN GEORGIA MOVEMENT

The story of Drawdown Georgia begins with Ray C. Anderson. The founder of Interface and a famed industrialist-turned-environmentalist, Anderson served as a Visionary Leader and Advocate for sustainable business. In 1994, Anderson set his flexible floorcoverings company on a path towards 'doing no harm'. The company's vision became known as 'Mission Zero': a commitment to eliminate any negative impact it had on the environment by the year 2020 (Anderson, 1998, 2010).

When Anderson passed away in 2011, his estate endowed a family foundation, the Ray C. Anderson Foundation. The foundation's purpose is to continue Anderson's legacy – specifically, to advance knowledge and innovation around environmental stewardship and sustainability. Through research and funding, the foundation aims to help create a better world for future generations. In the first years after its formation, the foundation created meaningful partnerships and funded innovative initiatives, including the Ray C. Anderson Center for Sustainable Business (ACSB) at the Georgia Tech Scheller College of Business.

In 2016, at an Advisory Board Meeting, some of the most accomplished environmental thought leaders gathered to help the family evaluate the impact their foundation had made in its short history. Against the backdrop of the environmental challenges facing society, the board members identified climate change as the most critical issue. Board Member Bob Fox said, 'I would go all-in on climate'. His words were immediately met by nods from around the table.

This meeting marked a turning point for the foundation. At the time, Executive Director John Lanier was a Board Member for Project Drawdown, a nascent nonprofit that was working to identify and quantify the world's most effective climate solutions. The nonprofit was led by Paul Hawken (also a member of the Foundation's Advisory Board). Hawken and his team were racing to complete their research and publish a book with their findings. The foundation decided to deepen its support for Project Drawdown.

Drawdown: The Most Comprehensive Plan Ever Proposed to Reverse Global Warming (Hawken, 2017) was published on 18 April 2017. It resonated with audiences because it showed how inclusive climate action could be. Solutions ranged from rooftop solar to reduced food waste, from carpooling to indigenous peoples' forest tenure, and from refrigerant management to bamboo production. The book showed that humanity has the tools at hand to successfully stabilize the climate. Just as important, it showed that everyone could do something to make a difference.

That said, not every solution is effective everywhere. *Drawdown* showed what climate solutions work best for the *planet.* Anderson's family found themselves wondering what climate solutions would work best for *Georgia,* their home state. Anderson had loved the phrase, 'brighten the corner where you are'. The foundation decided to go all-in on climate by doing just that.

The foundation convened a 'climate dream team' from Georgia's leading universities and nonprofits already working collaboratively on climate (see the Georgia Climate Project (GCP) callout box). The team decided to replicate the Project Drawdown model at a state level with two goals: (1) to figure out what climate solutions would work best in Georgia; and (2) to encourage the growth of those solutions.

Out of the conversations with the climate dream team, the Drawdown Georgia project was born. In 2019, the foundation committed to funding a research team spanning Georgia Tech, Emory University, Georgia State University, and the University of Georgia. The research team focused on the goal of identifying high-impact

The Georgia Climate Project. The GCP, which launched in 2016 (Rudd et al., 2018), is a state-wide consortium of 11 colleges and universities working to strengthen Georgia's ability to prepare for and respond to its changing climate. Its four strategic priorities are science, stronger conversations, solutions, and a stronger network. The statewide network created by the GCP and the prior collaborations among its members were instrumental in pulling together the multi-university Drawdown Georgia's team of experts. Working relationships forged through the GCP facilitated the launch of Drawdown Georgia, and its biennial state climate conferences have been a key platform for sharing progress and engaging stakeholders. In turn, the Drawdown Georgia roadmap of 20 solutions now provides structure to many of GCP's current activities and plans.

solutions for Georgia and estimating associated costs and benefits, while also considering how the solutions might impact societal priorities, such as economic development opportunities, public health, environmental benefits, and equity. Unlike many studies that focus on 2050, we chose to focus on making a difference by 2030.

As the multi-university team conducted their research over 18 months, the foundation developed a plan for encouraging the adoption and growth of the to-be-determined solutions. Foundation members realized that an academically rigorous set of climate solutions for the state would provide a valuable roadmap towards the destination of a zero carbon Georgia. The next key step would be to get people to take the journey. They believed that creating a movement would be essential to moving the needle on climate change in the state. Drawdown Georgia would need to inspire organizations, communities, and individuals to see themselves as essential participants in the mission to help the state reverse climate change.

At a tactical level, the building of a climate solutions movement has several layers. First, the foundation led the effort to create an attractive and inclusive Drawdown Georgia brand. Second, it invested in a robust communications apparatus to help share the research and tell the stories of Georgia's climate champions. Third, it repeatedly emphasizes the co-benefits of climate solutions (related to equity, health, the environment, and the economy), as these issues often motivate people more than facts about the amount of carbon in the atmosphere. Finally, it creates the space for others to lead – in congregations, cities and counties, higher education institutions, corporations, and more. Deep involvement from many individuals and organizations across the state will ensure that Drawdown Georgia succeeds.

2. IDENTIFYING A ROADMAP OF CLIMATE SOLUTIONS FOR GEORGIA

The commitment to partnerships infused the collaborative road mapping of climate solutions for Georgia. Four universities (Georgia Institute of Technology, Emory University, University of Georgia, and Georgia State University) worked with several nonprofit community organizations – Greenlink Analytics, the Partnership for Southern Equity (PSE), and the Southface Energy Institute – to design and implement the road mapping process. The goal was to create and deploy a replicable and science-based process that Georgia (and others) could use to identify high-impact climate solutions for a particular geography. The down-selection process began with the nearly 100 climate solutions identified by Project Drawdown as the most impactful global solutions (Hawken, 2017). These solutions were vetted by applying a sequence of filters covering their applicability to Georgia, technology readiness, magnitude of impact, cost-effectiveness, and beyond carbon attributes (health, economic development, ecosystem impacts, and equity). In the context of Georgia, which has large historical and ongoing inequities across demographic groups, the focus on equity was particularly important. Implementation pathways should not only mitigate existing injustices and institutional barriers to climate solutions but should also erase the inequities of access and benefit for future generations (Brown et al., 2021b).

For the diverse research team working across Georgia to be able to assess a wide range of technologies and so that the results could be easily compared, synthesized, and summarized, a common vocabulary and set of approaches and assumptions were developed. For example, historic greenhouse gas emissions (GHGs) and baseline forecasts for subsectors of the state's economy were quantified and illustrated in Sankey diagrams. This required the use of global warming potentials and CO_2 equivalencies (CO_2-e) for calculating the total impact of GHGs. Concepts such as the achievable and technical potential of climate solutions were also formalized (Table 8.1), along with the life cycle costs of implementing them using discount rates and planning horizons.

Georgia residents were polled via the Ray C. Anderson Foundation website to assess their views about the preliminary list of solutions, and five online Qualtrics surveys of stakeholders were

Table 8.1. Collaborative Research Requires the Development of Common Analytic Approaches.

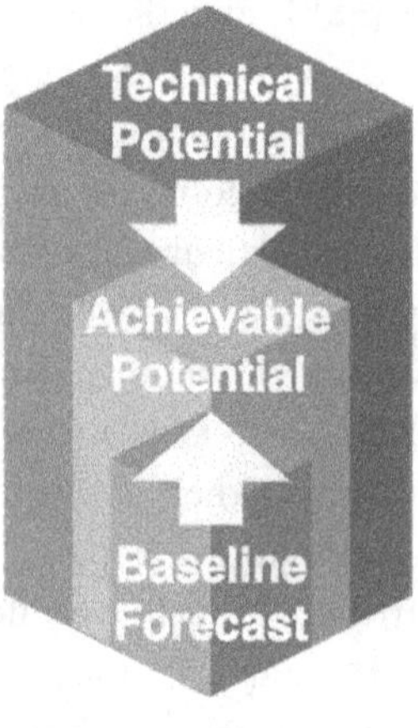

Technical Potential: Maximum realistic application without regard to cost or other impacts, up to hard limits on resources such as available land and materials (e.g. recycling 95% of disposed recyclable materials or covering 100% of south-facing and flat rooftops with solar panels)

Achievable Potential: A realistic scenario that considers costs, impacts, and stakeholder acceptance, but consistent with a greater commitment to success (e.g. EVs are 15% of new sales by 2030, growing large-scale solar from 1% to 11% of electricity)

Baseline Forecast: The 'no new action' scenario – status quo with slow change and continued trends conducted, covering each sector of the Georgia economy (Brown et al., 2021a). The information collected from this process was then discussed at an all-day workshop. Using plenary sessions and break-out groups, several hundred experts and stakeholders provided feedback about the preliminary down-select of solutions, which motivated a subsequent phase of research. To further inspire action and inform solutions, the Kendeda Building at Georgia Tech – one of 12 net zero buildings in the world – was chosen as the workshop venue (Fig. 8.1).

The final set of 20 high-impact solutions addresses a combination of traditional sources of GHGs from electricity generation, transportation, and the energy consumption of buildings (Figs. 8.2 and 8.3). In addition, the solutions tackle emissions from agriculture and food systems and focus on the carbon absorbed in trees and soils. These solutions are diverse and rely on different actors. Some solutions depend at least in part on the actions of consumers (e.g. rooftop solar, electric vehicles, recycling, plant-rich diets, and composting organic waste), others depend primarily on business

Fig. 8.1. Drawdown Georgia Workshop at Georgia Tech's Kendeda Building.

Credit: Copyright, Georgia Institute of Technology, photograph by Justin Chan, reprinted by permission.Dedicated in 2019, the Kendeda building is the first academic and research building in the Southeast to receive Living Building Certification from the International Living Future Institute. Its ability to generate more on-site electricity than it consumes, and to collect and treat more water than it uses, inspired the team to think big about the carbon drawdown possibilities for Georgia (Matisoff & Noonan, 2022).

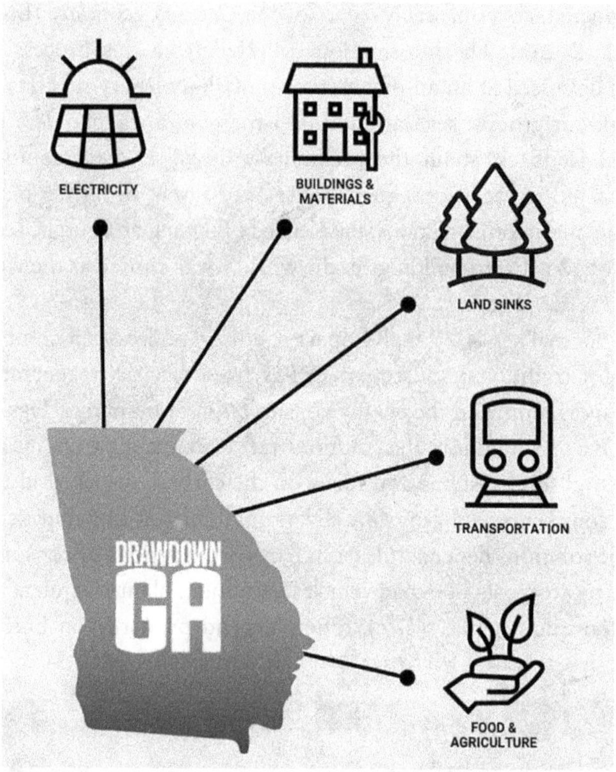

Fig. 8.2. Climate Solutions Come From All Sectors of the Economy.
Credit: Ray C. Anderson Foundation.

decisions (e.g. refrigerant management, conservation agriculture, increasing forest cover, and generating electricity from landfill methane). Some require significant public funding (e.g. mass transit), and all would benefit from private investments and supportive public policies. When considering the entire roadmap of 20 solutions, their interactions need to be considered. Synergies occur when the successful deployment of one solution magnifies the carbon reduction potential of another – as when electric vehicles use low carbon electricity from solar farms. Competitive effects also exist – as when homeowners self-generate their electricity from rooftop solar, which can reduce the carbon saved by energy-efficient appliances. The bottom line: Road mapping requires complex systems thinking.

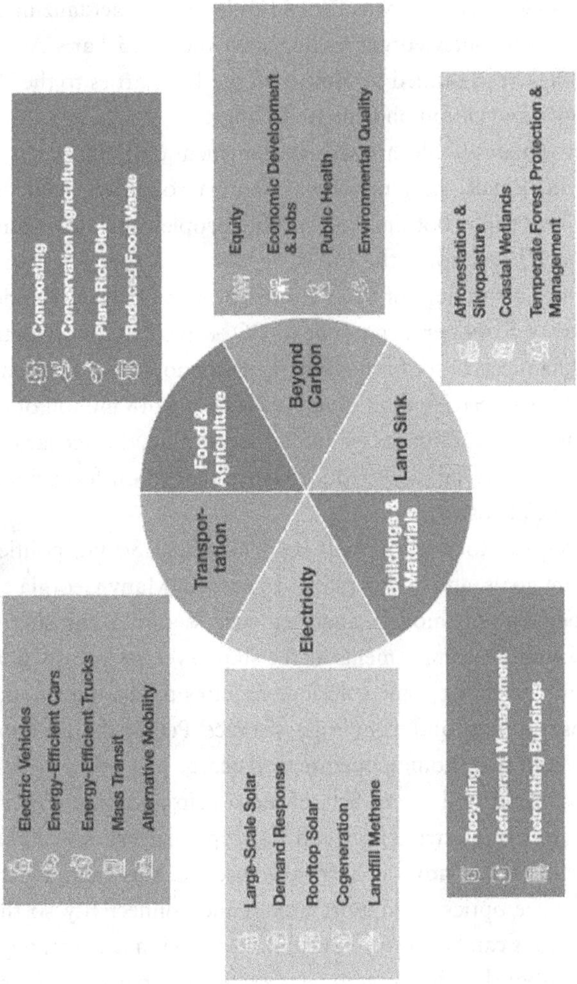

Fig. 8.3. 20 High-impact Climate Solutions for Georgia and Their 'Beyond Carbon' Attributes.

Credit: Marilyn Brown, Georgia Institute of Technology.

When all 20 abatement estimates are included and major interactions are considered, Georgia's GHG net emissions in 2030 are estimated to fall from the forecast of 122 to 79 megatonnes of CO_2-e (a 35% reduction). That would be a 50% reduction relative to Georgia's net emissions in 2005 (156.5 megatonnes). The Drawdown Georgia team was thrilled to learn that actualizing its roadmap would put Georgia in line with the 2015 Paris Agreement that has been ratified by almost all the 197 parties to the UN Framework Convention on Climate Change.

How much would all this carbon abatement cost? Brown et al. (2021b) show that the Drawdown Georgia roadmap would be good for the triple bottom line: profit, people, and the planet. Across the 20 solutions, the life cycle cost of abatement varies, ranging from net savings of $336 per megatonne of CO_2-e avoided to net costs of $144 per megatonne of CO_2-e avoided. In 2030, the estimated financial cost of following the Drawdown Georgia roadmap ranges from $1.3 billion of net benefits to $148 million of net costs. Thus, using traditional economic accounting, this scenario of 20 solutions could possibly reduce Georgia's carbon footprint at no net financial cost.

However, the total effort will be demanding. Strong political will, climate goals, and action plans are needed. Many Georgia cities have become role models, and their successes are being shared. However, without commitments at the state level, progress will be uneven. Implementing some solutions requires public information campaigns, training, and technical assistance. People do not know how to retrofit their homes, operate, and charge an electric vehicle, or compost their food waste. Schools need help understanding the pros and cons of electric buses and rooftop solar systems. Public funding is needed to advance infrastructures such as charging stations and fibre optics to support broadband connectivity so that smart solutions can be adopted in rural areas and in disadvantaged urban neighbourhoods. Government codes, standards, and procurement policies can encourage climate solutions. By focusing on near-term 2030 goals, pathways for policy action are becoming visible. Realizing these pathways remains a challenge. In contrast, business strategies that can scale the adoption of climate solutions in Georgia look promising. This was the impetus for the launch of a voluntary business coalition for climate action called the Drawdown Georgia Business Compact ('Business Compact').

3. LAUNCHING A VOLUNTARY BUSINESS COALITION FOR CLIMATE ACTION

The team unveiled the 20 high-impact solutions during Drawdown Georgia Launch Week in October 2020. At that point, the effort shifted to creating a movement for citizens and organizations alike to get involved in unlocking the significant value of regional decarbonization action (Hultman et al., 2020). A primary stakeholder group whose actions have significant impact at the local and regional level through its individual and collective commitments is the business community. The Ray C. ACSB at Georgia Tech's Scheller College of Business, whose vision is to 'empower tomorrow's leaders to create sustainable businesses and communities', took the lead in facilitating the creation of the Business Compact, a business-focused collaborative initiative focused on galvanizing climate action in Georgia.

3.1. Development of the Business Compact

ACSB's foundational work unfolded in three phases from October 2020 to October 2021: (i) baseline data analysis (use available data to develop a diverse list of companies and organizations to engage); (ii) best practice research and consultation (review literature and practice and undertake extensive stakeholder consultation regarding 'best fit' design for the Business Compact); and (iii) launch (finalize the Business Compact design and recruit members).

In the baseline data analysis, more than 40 companies that are either headquartered or have a physical presence in Georgia emerged as leaders in ambition and commitment for climate action based on the Science Based Targets initiative (SBTi) and Net Zero Tracker participation data as well as additional information on company sustainability commitments (Table 8.2). These companies each have science-based targets that align with a 1.5°C to-2°C trajectory for global warming and ambition similar to the

Table 8.2. More Than 40 Companies Headquartered and/or Operating in Georgia Have Set Ambitious, Science-based Carbon Reduction Targets.

Goals Align with 1.5°C		Goals Align with 2.0°C	
Accenture[b]	KPMG[a]	**Anthem**[b]	MEAG Power
Acuity Brands	Mercedes-Benz USA[a]	Cargill[a]	Porsche Cars North America[b]
Amazon[b]	Microsoft[b]	CEMEX[b]	Proctor & Gamble[b]
AT&T[b]	Morgan Stanley[a]	**Delta Air Lines**[b]	Saint-Gobain[b]
Ball Corporation[b]	Nestlé[b]	Home Depot[b]	**Southwire**
Cox Enterprises	Novelis[a]	**Kia Motors**[a]	Verescence[a]
Deloitte[a]	Owens-Corning[a]		
Emory Healthcare	Rubicon Global[a]		
EY[a]	Siemens[b]		
Facebook[b]	Skanska[b]		
General Mills[b]	SKC		
Google	Southern Company **(Atlanta Gas Light)**[a]		
Interface[a]	Symrise[a]		
JLL[b]	Walmart[b]		
Kimberly-Clark[b]	**YKK**[a]		

Note: The 1.5°C trajectory requires goals to halve GHG emissions before 2030 and achieve net zero emissions by 2050. The 2°C trajectory requires goals to reduce GHG emissions 40–70% (below 2010 levels) by 2050, achieve carbon neutrality by 2070, and achieve net zero emissions by 2100. Bolded companies represent Compact membership (as of 15 September 2022).

[a] Participation in SBTi or Net Zero Tracker Initiatives.

[b] Participation in both SBTi and Net Zero Tracker Initiatives.

Business Compact's goal to reduce carbon emissions to zero by 2050. Included within this leadership cohort are 11 Fortune 100 companies, six of the 50 largest employers in Georgia, and two of the six greatest large-facility emitters – Southern Company and

MEAG Power, which accounted for 49.35% and 5.16% of facility-level emissions in Georgia, respectively, according to 2019 USEPA FLIGHT data (U.S. Environmental Protection Agency Office of Atmospheric Programs, 2022).[1] The leadership of these companies in emission reduction goal setting is particularly significant given that nearly three-quarters of historical facility-level emissions in the state stem from power generation. A subset of the companies in Table 8.2, complemented by small- and medium-sized enterprises (SMEs) operating in different sectors and geographies within the state, were the focus of initial outreach and consultation regarding the Business Compact.

In recent years, the ambition and scope of climate-focused business coalitions (e.g. We Mean Business Coalition, Renewable Energy Buyers Alliance, and Net Zero 2050 Team) and campaigns/commitments (e.g. Business Ambition for 1.5C, SBTi, Race to Zero, We Are Still In, RE100, and EV100) have grown. A review of these initiatives showed that they all make a commitment to climate action that is guided by Intergovernmental Panel on Climate Change (IPCC) scenarios, that they emphasize public reporting, and that the coalitions have backbone organizations of varying sizes to advance signatories' joint agenda. Many of these consortia state that they are looking for forward-looking companies that aim to avoid climate change and create a safer, healthier world. The consortia are framed as a chance for companies in the highest emitting sectors to take action, reduce their environmental impact, and secure their financial stability and growth for the future.

Building on these findings, and based on workshops and one-on-one discussions with ACSB advisory board members and some of the companies in Table 8.2, the Business Compact's charter, membership principles, and primary activities were articulated as follows:

- *Commitment*: Companies joining the Business Compact are committing to taking individual and collective actions that support the statewide achievement of net zero emissions by 2050 through a just, competitive, and sustainable transition.

- *Membership Principles*: The Business Compact will be an inclusive platform that allows cross-sectoral participation spanning large corporations, SMEs (with an intentional focus on minority-owned businesses), start-ups, and service providers (e.g. financial services, IT companies, and utilities). Partners of the Business Compact will include leading non-governmental organizations (NGOs), chambers of commerce, technology, and other industry associations.

- *Activities*: The Business Compact will undertake the following activities that are facilitated by ACSB, which will serve as the backbone organization for the Business Compact:
    - *Create a Community of Practice*. ACSB will work closely with Business Compact participants, faculty in academic institutions, and partners to create a community of practice through collective learning experiences (e.g. workshops, dialogues, site visits, and student projects), shared knowledge and best practices, and other opportunities to support the objectives of the Business Compact and its members. It is anticipated that learnings and insights will be shared publicly.
    - *Facilitate Collaboration*. ACSB will develop and implement a process for identifying, vetting, and prioritizing collaborative projects on which Business Compact participants will consider taking action themselves (e.g. jointly participating in an afforestation program in the state). This process will be implemented in coordination with Business Compact participants, interested faculty members, as well as with NGOs, and others.
    - *Catalyze Innovation*. ACSB will help to design innovation platforms and/or collaborate with existing initiatives that connect thematically with the Drawdown Georgia solutions and net zero goals of the Business Compact. Discussion to date among Business Compact participants points to strong interest in grand challenges or other competitions focused on students, start-ups, and company/organizational employees.
    - *Report on Progress*. ACSB will work with participating companies and strategic partners to gather information and data that enables measurement and reporting on the impact

of collaborative efforts, such as contributions and progress towards the statewide target of net zero carbon emissions and other co-benefits like increasing equity and economic opportunity.

While the Business Compact shares similarities with other coalitions/commitments by design, it also has some unique features. First, it is specifically focused on the state of Georgia, which allows for solutions rooted in the local natural, economic, social, and regulatory context. Second, the research-based 20-solution menu allows for a diverse yet focused set of projects to emerge, and by continuing the collaborative Drawdown Georgia research program, the scientific and fact-based grounding of the Business Compact's activities is strengthened. Third, it has been conceived from the outset to be inclusive of not only large corporations but also a diversity of businesses and partners (NGO, academic, and government) and to be intentional about a just and equitable decarbonization pathway. This commitment is mirrored by the growing role of community-based organizations and Historically Black Colleges and Universities (HBCUs) in Drawdown Georgia's research program.

3.2. Business Compact Launch and Initial Activities

The Business Compact launched in October 2021 with 12 founding members. As of 30 July 2022, membership stands at 35, with others in various stages of discussion. Diversity among company industry, revenue, size, geography, urban versus rural location, and current carbon reduction efforts has been an important aspect of the initial recruitment and continued growth of the Business Compact. Of the companies identified as industry sustainability leaders in Table 8.2, 11 have joined the collective action initiative to date.[2] The 24 other Business Compact members were identified through relationships among Drawdown Georgia and ACSB and complement the major industry leaders by adding greater diversity in business size, sector, operating locations, and sustainability ambition level. For example, while the overrepresentation of the manufacturing sector within the Table 8.2 companies reflects the impact of manufacturing on scope 2 emissions, the Business Compact participation of Norfolk Southern and UPS elevate progress within the similarly high-emission transportation and warehousing industry. In addition, engagement of smaller businesses (e.g. Better Earth) alongside some of the state's largest employers (e.g. Cox Enterprises, Delta Air Lines, and The Coca-Cola Company) ensures diverse participation across Georgia's economy. By leveraging the Business Compact's diversity in developing and implementing initiatives, members' commitments can result in just and sustainable outcomes that honour COP26's reminder that equity, diversity, and inclusion are foundational to a just transition to net zero carbon emissions.

Since October 2021, focus has shifted to facilitated multi-stakeholder engagement to advance industry-led, high-impact solution adoption and scaling in Georgia. The work is organized according to the five solution areas of Drawdown Georgia, with Business Compact members self-selecting to be part of one or more working groups. In these working groups, participating companies collaborate to identify high-priority collective action projects. Initial project foci include resiliency in under-resourced neighbourhoods (Electricity subgroup), investment in carbon sequestration capacity in Georgia (Land Sinks subgroup), energy burden reduction for low- and moderate-income households (Built Environment and Materials subgroup), supporting vehicle electrification and expanded charging infrastructure (Transportation subgroup), and investing in local regenerative agriculture (Food and Agriculture subgroup).

3.3. From SMEs to MNEs: The Business Compact Forges a Path for Inclusive Climate Leadership

Georgia's economy draws strength from its proximity to markets, quality of life, and strong post-secondary education system. Yet it faces unprecedented challenges as global change affects cost of living, human migration, agriculture, sea levels, and more.

Corporate leaders must first understand the realities of the environment in which they work. Most leaders recognize that their products, talent, supply chains, and technologies must change substantially to succeed in the warmed economy. The best leaders are changing their companies fundamentally to make them part of the solution for the post-fossil fuel world.

The Business Compact provides a forum for business leaders to share ideas, learn best practices from peers, and take action as partners in the new industrial revolution. In Business Compact meetings, members discuss challenges and opportunities related to carbon abatement, new technologies, and the post-carbon economy. From its inception, the Business Compact, like Drawdown Georgia itself, was designed to welcome diverse members to the table, ranging from multinational enterprises (MNEs) to SMEs and entrepreneurs.

MNEs can make a large impact at a global scale – and Drawdown Georgia is keen to include the state's major businesses in its plan for collective action. SMEs and entrepreneurs play a vital role as well. Despite the Paris Climate Agreement, the United Nation (UN) SDGs, and climate action announcements from numerous corporations, global climate emissions continue to rise. Action is needed now. Everyone – and every type of organization – must be involved.

Business Compact leadership has been intentional about inclusion. All types of organizations will be affected by climate change and should be welcome to be a part of the solution. Also, while on one hand there are serious risks related to climate change, on the other hand there are significant business opportunities to be realized by the companies who innovate for the new economy. The Business Compact is working towards a net zero future while always keeping an eye on equity. Currently, over one-third of the 35 member organizations are small, start-up, or minority-owned businesses. Leadership continues on a deliberate path to expand Business Compact membership among these critical cohorts.

An inclusive Business Compact will help to ensure that small and start-up organizations, as well as those owned by historically underrepresented groups, are poised to enjoy the financial gains related to the new economy. After all, the market for the climate is heating up. According to TechCrunch, $40 billion was invested in climate-focused start-ups in 2021, more than double the investments made in 2020 (Kamps, 2022). The rise in capital infusion is promising for entrepreneurs focused on climate solutions. However, capital deployment is far from inclusive. Today, women receive less than 2% of all venture capital funding, women of colour receive less than 1%, and in 2022 the amount of overall funding going to Black founders dropped drastically from the funding deployed in 2021. This is not good enough. Climate change affects everyone; therefore, everyone should be able to provide solutions and reap the rewards for innovative solutions.

Sustainability is a mega trend with several drivers. Capital markets are betting big on companies that will be part of the climate solution and not part of the continuing problem. Indeed, investment capital is flowing out of old-generation industries (e.g. gasoline-powered cars) and into new ones (e.g. electric vehicles). Many investments target clean energy technologies delivered by research institutions (such as Georgia Tech) and early-stage technology companies. Behind the capital markets and research labs, consumers are demanding green energy, clean air, and refuge from an ever-growing number of global warming-driven natural disasters.

The Business Compact creates a space for forward-thinking business leaders to ideate and take action. These leaders are part of a new type of corporate outlook: one that is more holistic, more alert to upstream and downstream effects, and more willing to accept a broader responsibility for environmental and social impacts. This new way of business thinking cannot come too soon.

4. EXPANDING ON THE ISSUE OF EQUITY

The search for equitable climate solutions has always been front and centre in Drawdown Georgia, and it is continuing to gain traction. The 27th Conference of the Parties to the UN Climate Change Convention promises to address issues of climate justice, climate finance, adaptation, and climate damage, motivated in part by the publication of *Climate Change 2022: Impacts, Adaptation and Vulnerability* (IPCC, 2022). This report concluded that unequal societies are more vulnerable to the impacts of climate change and describes a vicious cycle. Climate change deepens inequality at the same time that inequality makes us more vulnerable to climate extremes. Project Drawdown's 'Drawdown Lift' shows how climate change 'intensifies the effects of poverty, inequality, population growth, rapid urbanization, and environmental degradation, and disrupts national economies and their long-term growth potential' (Jameel et al., 2022).

The equity profiling of climate solutions was initiated from the beginning of Drawdown Georgia's road mapping. This work forecasts public health benefits given the anticipated air quality improvements from displacing fossil fuels. Moreover, the transition away from coal in Georgia could greatly benefit the health of under-resourced populations because coal plants are often co-located near communities of colour. Less favourable equity issues were also uncovered. For example, rooftop solar, retrofitting, electric vehicles, and afforestation/silvopasture were found to have barriers to solution access and affordability. Many solutions also lack diverse workforces and business owners. 'Logic diagrams' were created for all 20 solutions, linking barriers and equity challenges to tools and opportunities in the ideation of a set of possible initiatives to expand equity-related benefits and mitigate potentially adverse impacts (see, e.g., Brown et al., 2021c).

It quickly became clear that these complex equity issues required greater attention. As is often the case in discussions about the deployment of solutions, front-line community leaders and groups were not sufficiently included in the initial stages of the work (Echoing Green, 2019). Acknowledging these gaps and critiques, the Drawdown Georgia Equity Opportunities Project (Scott et al., 2022) was launched to engage a broader array of Georgia front-line individuals in one-on-one conversations and focus groups to discuss pathways to equitable solutions. The work engaged the UN-designated Regional Centre of Expertise (RCE) Greater Atlanta (see the UN RCE callout box) and two of its action groups focused on Advancing Justice for All and Business Engagement, and tapped the expertise and management support from Georgia Tech's Serve-Learn-Sustain organization, ACSB, and the Drawdown Georgia Research Team.

RCE Greater Atlanta. Acknowledged by United Nations University in 2017, RCE Greater Atlanta is a regional sustainability network grounded in higher education that is committed to implementing the UN SDGs through education and training, with a particular emphasis on equity-focused dimensions and opportunities. It is one of over 180 Regional Centres of Expertise on Education for Sustainable Development that are part of a Global RCE Network. Spearheaded by the Georgia Institute of Technology, Emory University, and Spelman College and grounded in higher education, RCE Greater Atlanta brings universities and colleges from across Greater Atlanta together with nonprofit, community, government, and business partners. With its strong focus on equity and justice, the UN RCE, together with the Partnership for Southern Equity, were key contributors to the Drawdown Georgia Research Team's 'beyond carbon' work. The RCE empowers youth leaders in collaborating to have regional impact. A prime example is the UNITAR Youth and the SDGs e-learning course, developed by students from eight Atlanta higher education institutions to provide SDG training for youth from around the world (Hirsch et al., 2021).

Two subsets of solutions were examined in this project: (1) advancing carbon mitigation and equity through retrofitting, rooftop solar, and transit solutions; and (2) advancing carbon sequestration and equity through conservation agriculture and land sinks. Findings and recommendations emerged in several areas: historical factors limiting solution access, such as affordability, structural financial impediments, infrastructure challenges (e.g. lack of connectivity for rural farmers to engage in solutions), legal barriers, policy hurdles, and continuing racial bias. In addition, procedural equity emerged as an important theme and reminder for all climate-related initiatives to ensure greater community inclusivity, diversity, and engagement wherever possible in shaping climate-oriented initiatives.

The Business Compact is also working to centre equity considerations in the various climate solutions under consideration by Business Compact members, both in terms of potential projects and with respect to participation and inclusivity. In addition to Business Compact members, several nonprofit partners are supporting this work and proposing projects for Business Compact consideration.

In sum, Drawdown Georgia's replicable methodology advanced the science of carbon abatement by incorporating a partnership-intensive approach to road mapping. The team modelled solution interdependencies, spanning both carbon sources and sinks, clarified beyond carbon societal costs and benefits (including their distributional impacts), and engaged front-line leaders and groups to broaden the scope of concerns beyond those of traditional communities of scientific expertise.

5. LOOKING BACK AND LOOKING AHEAD

Since its beginning, Drawdown Georgia has moved ahead quickly on multiple fronts. The swift timeline can be attributed in part to the climate action foundation upon which Drawdown Georgia has been built. In the years leading up to the creation of the initiative, several relevant networks and activities had already matured in the state, including the Georgia Climate Project, RCE Greater Atlanta, the Carbon Reduction Challenge (see the callout box), and the ACSB Advisory Board, composed of climate leaders from corporations and NGOs. These networks and activities created the groundwork that enabled the Drawdown Georgia team to pull together a set of experts and advisors for the research. Participants in these established networks also provided business insights that helped to develop the operating principles and activities of the Business Compact. Early in the development of Drawdown Georgia, leadership acted on the realization that effective communications would be essential to deploying the results of research. From the beginning, Drawdown Georgia put a premium on standardized and attractive visualization (illustrated in Figs. 8.2 and 8.3). Science goes hand-in-hand with art that moves the human spirit. Drawdown Georgia effectively communicates through colourful photos of climate solutions, trackers of CO_2 sources and sinks, games that teach students the tools needed for climate problem-solving, and diagrams of complex financial analysis and equity issues. Through its arsenal of Ted Talks, YouTube videos, websites, and online collaboration spaces, Drawdown Georgia has introduced the climate crisis and solutions to people from all walks of life.

The robust climate action ecosystem in Georgia has developed in response to alarming predictions. Georgia and its Southern state neighbours are anticipated to be among states most adversely affected by climate change impacts across most major economic and related indicators such as GDP, mortality, and agricultural yields (Hsiang et al., 2017). Decarbonization is known to be the proper path forward, but many challenges must be faced and overcome: the sheer magnitude of a decarbonization transition, market uncertainties, a fragmented regulatory landscape, organizational capabilities of firms, the difficulty of pre-competitive cross-industry collaboration, the trade-offs between different environmental and social priorities, political polarization, and more.

The Carbon Reduction Challenge. The Challenge, an initiative of Georgia Tech's Global Change Program and ACSB, in collaboration with the Georgia Climate Project, is a competition focused on empowering students to become part of the climate change solution. Students from Greater Atlanta higher education institutions, sometimes working as individuals but most often in teams, are challenged to leverage their summer internships and co-ops to pitch their employer a project that achieves significant reductions in carbon emissions while delivering cost savings. Scores of companies, some of which are now Business Compact members, have hosted the interns and realized millions of pounds of CO_2 reductions and tens of thousands of dollars of cost savings. Oftentimes the projects deliver a suite of 'co-benefits', including reductions in air pollution that improve public health and greater employee satisfaction due to teleworking. Most importantly, the Carbon Reduction Challenge has endowed students – future business leaders, innovators, policy-makers, and more – with a transformative mindset. In 'Change 1% to Change the World' (TEDxGeorgiaTech Talks, 2018), former Challenge winner Will Courrèges-Clercq says: 'keep looking for short-term wins, [...] until your company reaches the level of transformation in its business model that allows it to make radical sustainability changes'.

While these challenges may seem daunting, Drawdown Georgia provides a state-specific roadmap towards success. It shows the state *how* to reach a net zero future. The question is: Who will join in the journey? Georgia's thriving business community, fortunately, is beginning to embrace the competitive opportunities associated with a transition to a low carbon economy. The state has numerous strengths to harness: for instance, being 8th in the United States in the number of Fortune 500 headquartered companies and home to leading startup metro areas such as Atlanta. A coalition of companies committed to a net zero future has the potential to move the needle significantly.

Looking forward, the Business Compact's goal is not only to increase the number of companies committed to carbon reduction but also to enhance and refine existing company carbon reduction commitments. By facilitating collaborations and developing a community of practice, the Business Compact will help more companies reach a maturity level where they set their first carbon emission targets. For companies with existing short-term emission reduction commitments, the Business Compact aims to support their progress in levelling up to long-term commitments. For companies that already have science-based targets, progress in their sustainability ambition may involve further exploring scope 3 targets or evaluating their efforts to support workforce transitions away from high-emitting industries to new business models. With each additional business commitment, the Business Compact advances individual and collective action that can result in positive local impact and progress towards tracking and achieving net zero emissions by 2050 in Georgia.

Drawdown Georgia also supports the belief that climate research in Georgia must be more inclusive and representative of the demography of Georgia. The state has one of the strongest networks of HBCUs in the nation, and Drawdown Georgia aspires to include those institutions deeply in engineering and analyzing climate solutions, as well as in the process of knowledge co-production. By integrating diverse knowledge and perspectives from traditional science, local communities, and management practitioners, knowledge co-production (Campbell et al., 2016; Sanchez Rodriguez et al., 2018) empowers individuals and communities who have been marginalized (Bixler et al., 2021). Well-developed, inclusive processes can structure relationships among science, society, business management, and policy-makers. This leads to more accurate and useful data and research results and increased buy-in to solutions that are people-centred and user-led (Audia et al., 2021). Drawdown Georgia has begun to work towards this goal by a bundling of philanthropic funding for climate solutions that engage diverse research performers.

As more parties become involved and the work of decarbonization is pursued, a main question is, *How will success towards goals be measured?* The Drawdown Georgia research program is turning to the creation of an interactive Solutions Tracker to visualize the adoption and use of solutions across the state, thereby promoting 'peer'suasion and solution activation. By linking the Emissions and Solutions Trackers, Drawdown Georgia will be able to spotlight notable shifts in emissions and connect solution activation to carbon drawdown. Altogether, this integrated set of activities will highlight opportunities for communities to enable local citizens, businesses, policy-makers, and NGOs to begin to answer the question 'What can we do to help?' and will lift up examples of climate solution implementation around the state. These tasks will engage Business Compact members. Through their communities of mutual interest and commitments to climate mitigation, Drawdown Georgia will continue to move solutions forward while documenting both progress and new emission reduction opportunities in the Solutions Tracker. Periodic information about the carbon reduction actions and solutions of Business Compact partners will be sought, which will in turn influence development of the Solutions Tracker.

Even if the initiative achieves its decarbonization goals, another question is, *Will it be enough?* The truth is, no matter what is achieved, we are likely facing a future with serious climate change risks. While Drawdown Georgia has been primarily focused on mitigation, in the future, the Business Compact may integrate adaptation into the Drawdown solutions. Climate scientists' predictions are occurring sooner than expected, with more frequent and more damaging climate disruption. As these effects grow in magnitude and impact, it becomes increasingly clear that Georgia must take steps to adapt to the effects of global warming. The Georgia economy, the well-being of its residents, and our ability to continue living on the land we occupy will depend on how well we adapt.

The twentieth century taught us that great problems ultimately yield to the application of talent, investment, and hard work. In the same spirit, we *can* forge a path forward to climate change solutions. In tomorrow's decarbonized economy, Americans will instal solar panels, erect windmills, build electric cars, and instal efficient home hot water heaters. This new economy will give birth to new markets, new opportunities, and growth. The new economy will be fuelled by more responsible capitalism.

Drawdown Georgia plots the path to get there – for the benefit of us all.

ACKNOWLEDGEMENTS

Funding for the Drawdown Georgia research and launching the Business Compact was provided by the Ray C. Anderson Foundation, whose staff and communications team have been instrumental to the development and success of Drawdown Georgia.

We thank the academic and community partners who have contributed to our collaborative research, our work on equity, and the creation of the Drawdown Georgia Business Compact. Our university collaborators have included: colleagues at Georgia Tech, the University of Georgia, Emory University, Georgia State University, Spelman College, and Agnes Scott College. Partners from community organizations include: Southface Institute, Greenlink Analytics, Partnership for Southern Equity, RCE Greater Atlanta, and Taproot. Members of the Drawdown Georgia Leadership Council have been sources of inspiration: their advice about priorities and opportunities has been insightful and much appreciated.

NOTES

1. Emissions across the state can be visualized in the GHG Emissions Tracker, which was launched by the Drawdown Georgia research program in 2022. The tracker enables concerned Georgia citizens, interested businesses, and policy-makers to identify county-level emissions. The tracker is being made even more relevant by downscaling to emissions from selected Georgia cities, accompanied by monthly updates and highlights of notable achievements across Georgia.

2. Bandwidth limitations and the desire to diversify initial membership in size, sector, geography, and ownership has meant that only a portion of these companies have been approached to join the Business Compact. Therefore, current non-participation on the part of a company does not imply a lack of interest.

REFERENCES

Anderson, R. C. (1998). *Mid-course correction: Toward a sustainable enterprise: The interface model.* Chelsea Green.

Anderson, R. C. (2010). *Confessions of a radical industrialist: How interface proved that you can build a successful business without destroying the planet.* Random House.

Audia, C., Berkhout, F., Owusu, G., Quayyum, Z., & Agyei-Mensah, S. (2021). Loops and building blocks: A knowledge co-production framework for equitable urban health. *Journal of Urban Health, 98*, 394–403. https://doi.org/10.1007/s11524-021-00531-4

Bixler, R. P., Yang, E., Richter, S. M., & Coudert, M. (2021). Boundary crossing for urban community resilience: A social vulnerability and multi-hazard approach in Austin, Texas, USA. *International Journal of Disaster Risk Reduction, 66*, 102613.

Brown, M. A., Beasley, B., Atalay, F., Cobb, K. M., Dwivedi, P., Hubbs, J., Iwaniec, D. M., Mani, S., Matisoff, D., Mohan, J. E., Mullen, J., Oxman, M., Rochberg, D., Rodgers, M., Shepherd, M., Simmons, R., Taylor, L., & Toktay, L. B. (2021a). Translating a global emission-reduction framework for subnational climate action: A case study from the state of Georgia. *Environmental Management*, *67*(2), 205–227. https://doi.org/10.1007/s00267-020-01406-1

Brown, M. A., Dwivedi, P., Mani, S., Matisoff, D., Mohan, J. E., Mullen, J., Oxman, M., Rodgers, M., Simmons, R., Beasley, B., & Polepeddi, L. (2021b). A framework for localizing global climate solutions and their carbon reduction potential. *Proceedings of the National Academy of Sciences*, *118*(31), e2100008118. https://doi.org/10.1073/pnas.2100008118

Brown, M. A., Hubbs, J., Xinyi Gu, V., & Cha, M. K. (2021c). Rooftop solar for all: Closing the gap between the technically possible and the achievable. *Energy Research & Social Science*, *80*, 102203. https://doi.org/10.1016/j.erss.2021.102203

Campbell, L. K., Svendsen, E. S., Roman, L. A. (2016). Knowledge co-production at the research–practice interface: Embedded case studies from urban forestry. *Environmental Management*, *57*, 1262–1280.

Echoing Green. (2019). *Growing a movement for justice: An examination of the sustainable development goals*. https://echoinggreen.org/news/growing-a-movement-for-justice-an-examination-of-the-sustainable-development-goals/

Hawken, P. (Ed.). (2017). *Drawdown: The most comprehensive plan ever proposed to reverse global warming*. Penguin.

Hirsch, J., Jelks, N. T. O., & Owokoniran, L. (2021). Reducing inequalities and empowering youth through the multi-stakeholder SDG network, RCE Greater Atlanta. *Sustainability and Climate Change*, *14*(3), 193–199. https://doi.org/10.1089/scc.2020.0079

Hsiang, S., Kopp, R., Jina, A., Rising, J., Delgado, M., Mohan, S., Rasmussen, D. J., Muir-Wood, R., Wilson, P., Oppenheimer, M., Larsen, K., & Houser, T. (2017). Estimating economic damage from climate change in the United States. *Science*, *356*(6345), 1362–1369.

Hultman, N. E., Clarke, L., Frisch, C., Kennedy, K., McJeon, H., Cyrs, T., & O'Neill, J. (2020). Fusing subnational with national climate action is central to decarbonization: The case of the United States. *Nature communications*, *11*(1), 1–10. https://doi.org/10.1038/s41467-020-18903-w

IPCC. (2022). Contribution of Working Group II to the Sixth Assessment Report of the Intergovernmental Panel on Climate Change. In H.-O. Pörtner, D. C. Roberts, M. Tignor, E. S. Poloczanska, K. Mintenbeck, A. Alegría, M. Craig, S. Langsdorf, S. Löschke, V. Möller, A. Okem, & B. Rama (Eds.), *Climate change 2022: Impacts, adaptation, and vulnerability*. Cambridge University Press. https://www.ipcc.ch/report/ar6/wg2/

Jameel, Y., Patrone, C. M., Patterson, K. P., & West, P. C. (2022). Climate–poverty connections: Opportunities for synergistic solutions at the intersection of planetary and human well-being. Project Drawdown. https://doi.org/10.55789/y2c0k2p2

Kamps, H. J. (2022, February 23). Climate investment is heating up with more than $40B invested across 600+ deals in 2021. TechCrunch. https://techcrunch.com/2022/02/23/climate-investment/.

Matisoff, D., & Noonan, D. (2022). *Ecolabels, innovation, and green market transformation: Learning to LEED*. Cambridge University Press.

Rudd, M. A., Moore, A. F., Rochberg, D., Bianchi-Fossati, L., Brown, M. A., D'Onofrio, D., Furman, C. A., Garcia, J., Jordan, B., Kline, J., Risse, L. M., Yager, P. L., Abbinett, J., Alber, M., Bell, J. E., Bhedwar, C., Cobb, K. M., Cohen, J., Cox, M., Dormer, M., et al. (2018). Climate research priorities for policy-makers, practitioners, and scientists in Georgia, USA. *Environmental Management*, 62, 190–209. https://doi.org/10.1007/s00267-018-1051-4

Sanchez Rodriguez, R., Urge-Vorsatz, D., & Barau, A. S. (2018). Sustainable development goals and climate change adaptation in cities. *Nature Climate Change*, *8*, 174–185.

Scott, A., Sherrod, N., Forbes, L., Ranson, H., & Pavlin, S. (2022). Drawdown Georgia equity opportunities project (V. A. Heard, M. Oxman, & R. Watts Hull, Eds.). Drawdown Georgia Research Report.

TEDxGeorgiaTech Talks. (2018). *Change 1 percent to change the world* [Will Courrèges-Clercq]. [YouTube]. https://www.youtube.com/watch?v=25BaNL7M6tA

U.S. Environmental Protection Agency Office of Atmospheric Programs. (2022). *Greenhouse Gas Reporting Program (GHGRP), Facility Level Information on GreenHouse Gases Tool (FLIGHT)*. www.epa.gov/ghgreporting

INDEX